Guideposts Personal Messages Of Inspiration And Faith

Guideposts

Books by Norman Vincent Peale

The Art of Living
You Can Win
A Guide to Confident Living
Not Death At All
     with Smiley Blanton, M.D.:
Faith Is the Answer
The Art of Real Happiness

GUIDEPOSTS

Personal Messages of Inspiration and Faith

Edited by

Norman Vincent Peale

PRENTICE-HALL, INC.

New York

To the men and women whose constant encouragement, co-operation, and counsel have unfailingly aided from the inception and throughout the development of the inspirational monthly publication, GUIDEPOSTS, this book is dedicated.

CONTENTS

ON MAKING RIGHT DECISIONS

HOME—CENTER OF HAPPINESS

IMPROVING YOUR COMMUNITY LIFE

INTRODUCTION TO GUIDEPOSTS

GUIDEPOSTS IS A COLLECTION OF INSPIRING, TRUE-LIFE EXPERI-
ences told by men and women of all faiths, in all walks of life.
Some of the most famous people in America—together with persons who drive our buses, carry our luggage, teach in our schools
and mingle with us on crowded sidewalks—relate personal incidents of how faith works in their lives. This book is packed with
moving examples of how a simple faith can bring out almost
incredible power and greatness in human beings.

It is *possible* to rise above disaster, overcome fear, break the
worry habit, convert handicaps into assets, solve seemingly impossible problems through religious experience. Men like Gene
Tunney, Eddie Rickenbacker, Harold Russell, and Sammy, the
Singing Bus Driver, have done just this. Others like Lowell
Thomas, Cecil deMille, J. C. Penney, J. Edgar Hoover, William
Green have been able to climb the ladder of success because they
had the "know-how" of applying religious principles in a practical
manner to everyday life situations.

Somewhere in this volume is a message or an experience that
will hit to the core of *your* problem, or to the problem of someone
close to you. People find great help and solace when they can
look at their problem objectively—through the similar experience
of another. Religion is the vital element in the lives of the men
and women whose personal stories make up this book. Their experiences may give you a fresh slant and a clarifying illumination
on your own problems.

Not only are the different situations that confront people herein
related, but also this volume shows *how* solutions may be arrived
at through simple religious formulas. Essentially the HOW of religion is stressed—HOW it can work for you as it has worked for
others. This volume presents a practical, workable, down-to-earth
religion for everybody.

Since 1944 these warm, human stories have been appearing in
GUIDEPOSTS, a non-profit, non-sectarian inspirational magazine
published at Pawling, New York. The experiences of our writers
who represent various faiths point up the fact that the important
thing about a person's religion is. Does he really believe and practice his own faith? Faith, your faith, will work when worked. Because of your belief in God your life can be happier and more
productive. Authors include Protestants, Catholics and Jews. Uni-
versal principles of faith are stressed In addition, men and women
of three faiths work side by side in the business and editorial offices
of GUIDEPOSTS. This publishing project therefore stands as a
symbol of the essential unity of all "believers."

The editors of GUIDEPOSTS wish to thank the authors included
in this volume for generously contributing their inspiring articles.
All royalties are applied to the expanding work of GUIDEPOSTS.
Famous personalities who could command large compensation for
their writings have generously donated their articles. They have
done so because they believe in the work that GUIDEPOSTS is
doing . . . the work of bringing about a better understanding
among members of all races, colors, and creeds . . . the work of
showing people that the only solution to the current ills of the
world is a resurgence of the same religious faith that gave our forefathers the strength and courage to meet and solve the problems
of their day.

The story of GUIDEPOSTS itself is the story of the faith and
determination of a few men. Raymond Thornburg, publisher,
originally conceived the idea of sharing the many stories that the
wonders of faith and prayer manifested in the lives of both great
and average people that I, as a minister, come to know. In an age
when civilization is considered more godless than believing, surely
these true experiences would have as much, if not greater, value
than any sermon preached. I agree wholeheartedly.

And so GUIDEPOSTS was born in Pawling, New York, back in
1944. Lowell Thomas, Captain Eddie Rickenbacker, Branch
Rickey, Stanley Kresge, Walter Teagle, J. Howard Pew, William
Banks and men of similar character and standing sponsored
GUIDEPOSTS, a monthly personal-experience publication, contain-
ing signed, exclusive stories written in a plain-talk way by business

and professional leaders and by people in all walks of life—the "man in the street."

The response has been beyond our hopes. No matter how famous or how busy, men and women have given freely and generously of precious time and work and confidences in order to share the joy and benefits that they have reaped from their earnest search for a greater understanding of God. Others have given financial aid, practical advice, voluntary work in long and faithful service, credit and patience, art and technical help, and business and accounting guidance.

Readers have heartened us with their hungry interest. The amount of mail from people who have been helped by GUIDEPOSTS' articles is very large. Now, recognizing the service that GUIDE-POSTS supplies to the evident need and desire of the reading public, we have assembled a varied selection of fifty-two out of some 116 articles for a volume of practical, spiritual aid.

Much credit for the success of GUIDEPOSTS in the past two years is due to the addition to my staff of Frederic C. Decker, Managing Director, Len LeSourd, Associate Editor, and Grace Perkins Oursler, Executive Editor, in the order in which they joined the organization Nor can I sufficiently thank John J. Hill, Jr., for his invaluable assistance with our art work and make-up, Jack Ferrara for his work on our Calendar of Holy Days and Holidays of Protestants, Catholics and Jews, and Otto Frankfurter who has been an advisory editor and mentor and friend. Appreciation also goes to our faithful office staff.

How to use this book—I suggest that you keep it on your night table Open at random or consult the Contents for an article to suit your mood. Read one (one a day is sufficient)—then offer a little prayer of affirmation saying "God is here with me. He is watching over me this night. Tomorrow He will guide me and give me all the strength I need He is now filling my mind, my heart, my body with peace and power."

So saying turn out the light and conceive of the faith about which you have read as permeating your subconscious mind, driving deep to the very center of your life. Do this once each day and this book will indeed become *your* guidepost to happier, more efficient living.   —Norman Vincent Peale

Throwing off Your Fears

YOUR FAITH
CAN KNOCK OUT FEAR

by

Gene Tunney

Gene Tunney twice pounded out fistic victories over that great pugilist, Jack Dempsey, but his greatest knockout was scored over his own fears. During the recent war Gene organized the Navy's physical fitness program. He is also author of the book Arms For The Living.

I WAS ONE SCARED YOUNG MAN ON THE MORNING OF THE NEW Year in 1920 The opponent whom I was scheduled to box that afternoon was a tough veteran named Whitey Allen, as cagey and experienced a fighter as they come.

It was one of my first bouts since returning from France where I had served as a Marine in World War I. I was still wet behind the ears in the professional fighting sense. My fear on this day was based on a fear that I'd had all my life—of professionals.

I can remember praying that morning as fervently and humbly as any man ever has. I prayed that in the fight that afternoon I might not be permanently injured when I was knocked out. I didn't ask that I might win. I took it for granted that I'd be knocked out, and I was terribly afraid of being hurt for life.

The prize ring is a rather terrifying place when you think about it. You're up on a raised platform which is a glare of light. All around you is the dim expanse of the crowd. You see faces wrenched with expressions of frantic excitement, emotions pro-

[3]

duced by the lust for battle—gloating, savage mouths open with yelling.

In every fighter comes occasionally the supreme horror of not being able to fend off the blows showered on him, of being helpless to raise his hands to ward them off.

Thus when I prayed that I might not be permanently injured, I gained confidence that I wouldn't be This took the edge off mad, irrational fear. If it hadn't been for this confidence I gained from prayer, I imagine that I'd have gone into the ring inwardly shaking and quaking, thoroughly beaten in advance.

As it was, I climbed into the ring that day with enough courage to go through the orthodox procedures of fighting a normal fight. In the second round I suddenly realized how groundless my fears had been. My opponent was no super-man. I went on to win the fight.

Thus I had scored one victory over fear. But years later faintness of heart nearly cheated me out of the championship.

This happened before my title bout with Jack Dempsey. Dempsey, the Manassa Mauler, was an overwhelming favorite to thump me out in an early round. Newspapers talked of what a murderous lacing he would give me. Being human I read the papers to find out what they were saying about me.

One night at the beginning of my long training period I awakened suddenly and felt my bed shaking. It seemed fantastic. Ghosts or what? Then I understood. It was I who was shaking, trembling so hard that I made the bed tremble. I was that much afraid—afraid of what Dempsey would do to me. The fear was lurking in the back of my mind and had set me quaking in my sleep, the nightmare thought of myself being beaten down by Dempsey's shattering punches.

The vision was of myself, bleeding, mauled and helpless, sinking to the canvas and being counted out. I couldn't stop trembling. Right there I had already lost that ring match which meant everything to me—the championship. I had lost it—unless I could regain it.

I got up and took stock of myself. What could I do about this terror? I could guess the cause. I had been thinking about the fight in the wrong way. I had been reading the newspapers, and all they had said was how Tunney would lose. Through the newspapers I was losing the battle in my own mind.

Part of the solution was obvious. Stop reading the papers. Stop thinking of the Dempsey menace, Jack's killing punch and ferocity of attack. I simply had to close the doors of my mind to destructive thoughts—and divert my thinking to other things. It took discipline. And again prayer and faith were pillars of strength to me.

This was the right medicine since I did go out and beat Dempsey in two straight fights. And the one moment when I was closest to defeat—I had been knocked to the canvas for a count of nine—produced the most humorous touch. Father Francis Duffy, the great World War I chaplain of the Fighting Sixty-ninth, and a close friend of mine, was at the fight. Sitting behind him was a very demonstrative young man. When I was lying dazed on the canvas, this young fellow went wild with excitement and noticing that Father Duffy, sitting in front of him, was a priest, pounded him violently on the back.

"Father, for Judas' sake, pray for Gene."

Father Duffy told me afterward that he instinctively began to pray, not that I would win over my opponent, of course, but that I would do my best and deliver to the fullest extent of my powers. Right, Father! That's the prayer of a sportsman.

I wonder how many millions of people face similar fears in their own lives. Not necessarily fears of physical nature either. Perhaps they too have been thinking too destructive thoughts.

A simple illustration is that of a man who is afraid of losing his job. He dwells on the imaginary scornful remarks his friends will make, the loss of face. Soon he visualizes a completely pitiful picture of himself. And it is more than likely in this case he will lose his job because of such negative thinking.

From my experience in two world wars I can also say that fear is the dominant emotion of a soldier. He fights his terror, dwells on it and it only increases. But how to get one's mind off fear? Religious fervor is a state of feeling like fear, and there are age-old exercises for stirring an ardor of faith.

The principal of these is prayer. You can pray away your terrors, if you have enough faith. You can become spiritually exalted instead of afraid. Religious emotion can take the place of fear.

I speak of the practical necessity of faith and prayer, because that's the part about which I know the most; I know it from experience. I speak as one to whom religious belief has been a life-long resource—this in a life given so largely to a career of fighting. I know faith and prayer as creative forces for courage.

These personal experiences have made me value the belief, the traditional worship and the church in which I was reared. They also made me more hostile to the dark anti-religious forces that would destroy the happiness and the wonder of the faith of ages.

I recall a beautiful expression of John McCormack, the great lyric master of song. During my visit to Ireland I had an opportunity to see a great deal of him. His favorite expression, striking, characteristic, was a parting good-bye "May God keep you in the palm of His hand," he would say with all the melody of an Irish brogue. In it was all the folklore flavor of Irish mysticism, that sense of intimacy of the Divine, enjoying the friendship of God. An expression too of simple faith in the goodly order of the universe.

DON'T BE AFRAID

by

Henry J. Taylor

"I left the world for the first time in my life when, as a boy, I took a trip into the coal mines," Henry J. Taylor relates "But my father calmed me and gave me a formula for conquering fear that has guided me all my life." Mr Taylor, journalist, economist and author of many books including Men In Motion, *is highly popular as a radio commentator.*

HURTLING DOWN A MINE SHAFT WITH MY FATHER WHEN I WAS A small boy, I discovered for the first time what God is like This was one of the most vivid of my boyhood experiences, my first trip down into a coal mine. My father's mine was in the process of having an elevator or cage installed so we had to make the descent in a barrel.

Father got in the barrel first, reached over and lifted me in. The cable swung the barrel out and over the center of the dark shaft, twisting us around and around as it dangled there. All I could see below was blackness and a tiny light at the bottom. The engineman threw a lever.

We started to drop. In an instant the white-blue of the sky was gone Father held me tight in his arms. My heart was beating like a trip hammer. My little world of time and space and the things I knew and could see had suddenly been whisked away, as though some giant hand had snatched it from around me.

I had left the world for the first time in my life. The only reality was what my fingers could touch. All else had ceased to exist.

[7]

But my father was there. I felt him in the darkness. We were dropping very fast in the rush of air. As the cage shot down in the darkness, banging hard against the wet, black walls, I could hardly catch my breath.

"Don't be afraid, son," he said. The speed of the cage diminished. A pressure came in my ears, and I swallowed hard. A second later the black wall of the shaft before me suddenly gave way and we came to a stop at the bottom of the mine. Father lifted me out of the barrel. I was as bewildered as a boy could be, I just stood there, clung to father's hand, and wondered what could possibly happen next.

The low, black roof, closely beamed with timbers, stretched into the darkness Thin tongues of yellow flames, spurting from the diggers' pit lamps, marked men working in the distance, but didn't disclose them It was as quiet as a mausoleum. I could hear only the steady trickle of the mine seepage, water dropping on loose rock, and father's breathing near me.

Then he lit a kerosene torch, the flame blown forward by the downcoming current of air from the shaft behind us. He took a better grip on my hand in the dark and told me to follow him. Stooping low, the shale roof pressing down on us and the walls of coal pressing in on us in the darkness, father led the way along the tunnel towards the yellow dots of light.

I could walk straight up, and this was much easier. As we got further into the mine, the air grew thick with the mist of fine coal dust. The mud was deep and very heavy. Two lights ahead appeared larger than the others, and from their jerky motion I knew the men were coming towards us before I could hear their feet thumping over the ties of the work track. The little lights bobbed closer, grew larger.

Then below the lights I could see the body of a man stripped to the waist, a black coating of dust that was moist with gleaming streaks of sweat. The other light was on the head of an animal. He was leading a mule.

"Look out for gas," the miner said to father, not even seeing me behind him in the darkness. "There's a bit here up high."

He lifted the lamp slowly to the jagged roof. A quick, blue flame suddenly extended from the lamp and puffed gently at him as he took his hand away.

I was so astonished I could hardly speak.

There in the mine someone asked me if I was afraid and I remember saying, "Well, I'd be awfully scared except my father is with me."

I remember my father looking at me with a grave and yet wonderful smile and saying, "Then you will never be scared, son, because a Greater Father than I will always be with you."

When I was a boy, my father gave me this advice. "Don't worry too much about yourself and about getting hurt. People who go through life being very cautious miss a great deal. Take your chances whenever you have to. It's better luck, you'll see more, and you'll probably live as long anyway."

I never forgot those words.

My father lived his life according to these principles. His primary attribute was his own self-faith, and out of this self-faith and his clear vision, he left home as a young man with three hundred dollars and an idea. In several years he had a partnership in a vast coal business.

America abounds with such men. Their credit is character. Their funds are faith in God and plain hard work. Their purpose is the American way of life.

As the years went on, father's interests widened, but his heart remained married to his mine operation. Nothing was too good for that mine—or the men who worked for him. And any man could write his own ticket when it came time for him to quit.

Take Matt Keefer for example. Matt had always tended to the mules, but his time was drawing near. He had trouble with his eyes and was slowly going blind. Matt was all through, but father simply couldn't tell him so.

Then father bought a farm near the mine as a surprise for

Matt. He built a house on it, barns and all, but kept off the subject of Matt's eyes until the gift was ready.

One day the whole place was in apple-pie order. Father then took Matt by the arm and walked him down the road. They stopped in front of the gate where Matt's two sons were waiting. Then father whirled the big mule skinner around and grabbed him by the shoulders.

"Matt," he said, "you're the best muleman in all the world, but you've just become a farmer. God bless you."

Great hulking Matt Keefer cried like a baby.

My father not only taught me the basic values—integrity, courage, tolerance, faith in God—he set examples in his own life that were much more effective than teaching me with words. From my earliest memory he brought me in contact with many great things that were happening in the world, to make me feel the throbbing growth of America.

No matter how dark and fearsome things become I never forget my father's words while hurtling down that mine shaft, "Don't be afraid, son," and I wasn't afraid for he was there The same confidence expanded to a mature spiritual faith will remove fear from our hearts. It will lead us to a true understanding and mastery of the confusing forces of this world.

I DARE YOU

by

William H. Danforth

*Meet the tingling challenge of William H. Dan-
forth, whose dynamic principles outlined here
have fired many a person to great achievement.
Mr Danforth is Chairman of the Board of the Ralston Purina Company of St Louis and one of the
business leaders of America.*

As a boy I lived in a rural community surrounded by swamp
lands. Those were my days of chills and fever. When I came to
school in the city I was sallow-cheeked and hollow-chested. One
day in class a very discerning teacher, who was a health crank,
turned and looked straight at me.

"I Dare You to be the healthiest boy in the class," he said, with
flashing eyes and emphasis on the *Dare*.

This brought me up with a jar. The other boys were all more
robust. I was a sick specimen who really needed a friend. My
teacher continued·

"I Dare You to fill your body with fresh air, wholesome food,
and faithfully exercise every day until your cheeks are rosy, your
chest full and your limbs sturdy."

His voice tingled every fiber inside me. My blood was up. The
Dare gripped me I was challenged to be as strong as any of the
fifty-two boys in that class. Today, sixty-two years later, there are
only two of that class living and the sickest boy of all is one of
them.

I once read of a mother who took an axe to a bear that
threatened her baby. A mother cannot kill a bear—*but this one did.*

[11]

I believe we have within us hidden forces, sleeping giants which, when aroused, stir us to perform amazing feats. In our lives there are four such forces. I call them the Physical, the Mental, the Social and the Religious. They form the four sides of my square. Life becomes complete when we develop each side. Down through the pages of history great men have been telling us the secret of Four Square living.

Listen to Sir Wilfred Grenfell's message: "Man must play, work, love and worship to get the most out of life." A body, a brain, a heart and a soul—the Four Square life again.

Why is it that a sickly boy can become a healthy one just because of a Dare? If it can happen to me, can't it happen to you also? Try it. Let's apply this Dare idea to life and watch the results —the weak become strong, the timid bold, the dull sparkling. I have tried the Dare idea on my associates with remarkable results so I am challenging you to try it.

I Dare You to STAND TALL . . . to be strong.

My boyhood experience proved to me that any one can become strong. First you must want to be healthy. It costs a little, but good health is worth a price. Who wants to be a little runt? STAND TALL —Stretch Now breathe deep. Bend over until the tips of your fingers touch the floor. Do it fifty times. Now the liver-squeezer, twisting around—back and forth fifty times. Do you like it? I don't. I hate exercise, but exercise is good for me, and I'm going to take it religiously night and morning. Make it a daily habit. Never fail. It puts a glow in your cheeks Keep it up from now on—*Yes, from now on.* Stand Tall.

I Dare You to THINK TALL . . . think creatively.

The world needs long-range thinkers. Ideas are the dynamos that move civilization. After a lifetime in business, I have never seen such a demand for ideas. Why sit back and wait for yourself to be adapted to the changing world when you can be one of those who will help bring about these changes? Develop a program of worthwhile daily reading if you would Think Tall.

I Dare You to SMILE TALL . . . to develop a magnetic personality.

Many a time I have seen country boys, too timid to interview prospective customers, develop into successful executives because of exceptional ability to get along with people. I know, because I have dared many of them to become real personalities. Here are a few Dares through which I have tried to measure myself:

I Dare You, Winning Smile, to replace Old Man Grouch.

I Dare You, Flabby Fingers, to develop into a Warm Handclasp.

I Dare You, Mr Snapping Turtle, to depart to another climate.

I Dare You, My Own Personality, to become a Welcome Guest.

The development of friendship is the enlargement of personality. Look for the best in people. Learn to like people. Select five new persons this week and determine to share your best self with them

I Dare You to LIVE TALL . . . to build character.

It is to you, strong of body, brilliant of mind, magnetic in personality, that I am talking now. What price all of these without the inspiration of a Cause? If attack is the keynote of growth in our Physical, Mental and Social lives, why not in the Spiritual, too?

Religious growth requires action, the doing of right things instead of wrong. We advance by doing. You may say your prayers tonight, but unless you can act on them tomorrow they are not worth much.

Take this incident that occurred in the rugged Himalayas. The driver of a bus was about to start out over one of the worst winding roads in the world. He was nervous, so before starting out he came in front of the engine and stood with folded hands, saying his prayers to the machine. That done, he began the journey, but had not gone far when the engine began to overheat. There was no water in the radiator.

This was remedied. When he had proceeded but a little way farther the machine stopped on a hill. He had run out of gasoline. Passengers and driver were stuck until rescued. The driver had said his prayers to the machine, but had put no water in the radiator and no gas in the tank.

To Live Tall is to put ourselves in the hands of the Supreme Being and make our religion a daily adventure. Preachers like Paul and Peter, Medical Missionaries like Grenfell, and humble men of faith everywhere have found that religion is a power that works in every condition of life.

What is spiritual adventure, you may ask?

In St Paul's Cathedral, London, on a tablet in memory of General Charles Gordon, I read these immortal words:

> "Who at all times and everywhere gave
> His Strength to the Weak
> His Substance to the Poor
> His Sympathy to the Suffering
> His Heart to God."

That is spiritual adventure.

Finally—I Dare You to live in the Presence of the Best. Try for one week to surround yourself with the best in life. Read an excellent poem Begin the biography of a distinguished man. Study a painting of an old master. Hear a best Victrola record. Listen to a symphony. See an uplifting play Hear a stirring speaker. Meet an inspiring personality. See a sunrise and sunset. Surround yourself with the world's excellence, and you can live like a king. I Dare You!

Prayer in Time of Need

I BELIEVE IN PRAYER

by

Eddie Rickenbacker

Captain Eddie Rickenbacker is high on the list
of America's heroes A man of inspired and demon-
strated faith, he has become in his lifetime almost a
legendary figure. He is president of Eastern Air
Lines, and one of the country's most vital and ac-
tive business leaders.

THERE ARE A LOT OF THINGS ABOUT THE HUMAN MIND AND SOUL
that we don't know much about. We get glimpses of them when
in times of danger or suffering we cross a little way over the line
of ordinary thought.

As I roared down the last stretch in an automobile race years
ago, I felt that I could control that machine with my mind, that I
could hold it together with my mind, and that if it finally collapsed I could run it with my mind. It was a feeling of mastery, of
supreme confidence. But it was real.

If I had said such a thing then, the boys would have called me
crazy. Even now I can't explain it. But I believe that if you *think*
disaster you will get it Brood about death, and you hasten your
demise. Think positively and masterfully, with confidence and
faith, and life becomes more secure, more fraught with action,
richer in achievement and experience.

Perhaps such things as the control of mind over matter and the
transmission of thought waves are tied up together, part of something so big we haven't grasped it yet. It's part of us and part of
the Something that is looking after us. It's one of the things that

make me believe in personal protection and in life after death. I
don't know how to put it into words.

Another strange thing happened to me. Several years ago I was
flying to Chicago. It was a Sunday afternoon in the middle of De-
cember, and the weather was miserable. There was a lot of ice.
We suddenly lost the radio beam. For a long time we cruised back
and forth trying to pick it up. Fog was all around us. We were
lost, off the beam, and flying blind Our two-way radio went out,
and we had lost all communication with the world. For seven
hours we flew—where, we didn't know. Nobody knew where we
were; nobody even knew we were lost.

Darkness was coming on. Then, suddenly, we saw a break in
the murk. The pilot brought the ship down to within one hundred
feet, and we saw lights go flashing by on a four-lane highway.

"It must be going from some place to some place," I said, and
we followed it for some distance.

Then we saw a red glow away off to the right, headed for it, and
saw a river gleaming. We flew up that river, and out of the six-
thirty dusk of winter sprang a town—Toledo! I saw the Toledo-
Edison sign flashing as we swept over the bridge tops. Skimming
the roofs, we circled and landed at the airport a moment later. We
had just enough gas left for eleven minutes of flight.

We had flown blind, without a beam, but we were on a beam,
just the same. I like to think it was the "Big Radio" that kept us
going—the Thing that keeps all of us flying safely through the fog
and night, toward some mysterious and important goal. The "Big
Radio" is a two-way job. You've got to keep tuned with It, and
you have to talk back. I believe in prayer. I learned to pray as a kid
at my mother's knee.

One day in France, with only one magneto on my Nieuport
biplane functioning, I was attacked by three German Albatross
planes. I came out of a dive so fast that the terrific pressure collapsed my right-hand upper wing. No matter what I tried I
couldn't come out of that whirl of death. I often wish I could
think as fast under normal conditions as I did during that drop.

While I fought the controls and tried to get the engine going, I saw all the good and bad things I had ever done, and most of them were bad. Then I began to pray.

"Oh, God," I said, "help me get out of this."

As a last desperate act, I threw my weight to the left-hand side over the cockpit and jammed the controls, then jammed the engine wide open. The thing suddenly sputtered and vibrated violently, and sailed away on her one good wing for France. I held it that way all the way home.

This escape and others I have had were not the result of any super-ability or super-knowledge on my part. I wouldn't be alive if I had to depend on that. I realized then, as I headed for France on one wing, that there had to be Something Else. I had seen others die—brighter and more able than I I knew there was a Power. I believe in calling upon It for help.

I am not such an egoist as to believe that God has spared me because I am I. I believe there is work for me to do, and I am spared to do it, just as you are. If I die tomorrow. I do not fear the prospect at all.

On a rainy night in February, 1941, I had the worst accident of my life. As I look back on those agonizing days in the hospital, I realize there was a reason behind it all. It was a test and a preparation for what was to follow.

In the four months I lay in that hospital I did more thinking about life and death than I had ever done before. Twenty-one months later, I was adrift in an open lifeboat with seven other starving men, most of them so young they needed the strength and understanding of a man who had been down in the valley of the shadow, who had suffered and made sense out of his suffering. To those men I was able to bring the essence of the religion and philosophy I had distilled in the hospital.

Once I almost died from a throat hemorrhage.

"Here," I said, "is death."

It dawned upon me in a flash that the easiest thing in the world is to die, the hardest is to live. Dying was a sensuous pleasure; liv-

ing was a grim task. In that moment I chose to live. I knew from
experience that abandonment to death was a sin. I was quitting. I
had work to do, others to serve.

Many things came to me. I realized I wasn't *afraid* to die, because I have lived so much in good ways and bad that I no longer
feel the youthful pang of not having lived at all. I knew only the
sorrow of being unable any more to help other people. And when
I finally came around, I saw life and death and the meaning of
the Golden Rule more clearly than I had ever known.

I took that clarity with me to the rubber raft in the South Pacific after our plane crashed. I shall not recount that story again.
I merely want to tell you the meaning of it. Of the eight men in
those three rafts, I alone never lost faith that we would be picked
up. Throughout those twenty-one days of blistering sun and
nights of ghastly chill, we were adrift for a purpose. I saw life had
no meaning except in terms of *helping* others.

I humbly think man instinctively does not interest himself in
others. He does it by an act of will. He sees that "*I am my brother's
keeper*" and "*Do unto others*" are the essence of all truth.

My experiences and the suffering through which I passed
taught me that faith in God is the answer to life.

Recently, in a rehabilitation hospital, I addressed a group of
disabled veterans. Many were discouraged; the future looked
dark and unpromising. I knew how they felt . . . I too had been
through a lot, but had found a secret which brought me through,
and I urged them to find the same secret.

I said, "If you have not had an experience of God in your life,
my advice is to get busy and get yourself one." For that is the sure
way to win victories over inner defeat. It is the way a humble man
meets life or death.

MIRACLE IN MY CLASSROOM

by

Ruth Moulton

*"Teaching school regardless of pay is a marvel-
ous life. I hated to give it up," stated Ruth Moulton upon retiring recently. Here she vividly tells of
her most thrilling experience of forty-four years of
service.*

I BRACED MYSELF FOR A DIFFICULT INTERVIEW. BEFORE ME, I
felt sure, was another of those demanding mothers. Something in
the way the woman had shut the door and then looked so carefully
around her brought back unpleasant memories of other talks during which special requests had been made of me as headmistress
of the school.

"Sara," the mother began—then stopped. I found myself tapping the desk quietly with the rubber end of my pencil.

"Sara," the mother repeated, now with an obvious effort, "is
going blind." She bit her lip.

"Oh, I *am* sorry." A wave of sympathy flooded me. "Are you
sure?" I asked with feeling.

"Yes, we're quite sure. The doctor calls it 'progressive near-
sightedness.' Of course the child must never know. You must help
there—and also keep her out-of-doors as much as your routine will
allow."

I nodded quickly. "Here in the country we can easily see to
that. I'll make a special point of it in Sara's case. I'm so very sorry

about it all . . . it does seem . . ." I stopped helplessly and we
looked at each other fixedly for a moment.

"I'm a great believer in prayer, you know," I continued. "Take
time for it every morning. We must pray over *this*"

A slight look of hopelessness flickered over the mother's face.
She arose, grasped my hand firmly and then left my office

It was a golden September day outside. The school year had
just commenced for some 125 students in this college preparatory
school for girls run by my husband and myself. Already I had a
problem case to worry about.

I immediately made a point to become acquainted with Sara.
She turned out to be a cheerful, very active of girl of fourteen—
but a bit too earnest for her years. Hardly taking time to adjust
herself to the new school, Sara plunged quickly into her studies
with eager, almost startling intensity.

I kept my word. From then on Sara was constantly in my
prayers.

One autumn morning the weather was so clear and warm that
I decided to walk up to a nearby hillside for early morning prayer.
On this hill next to the school I had often found God's presence
so real that I gained fresh insight into His will for the school. I
had been there but a few moments when the sound of footsteps
startled me. Looking up I saw Sara coming down the path from a
point still higher up the slope.

"Why, Sara," I called, "you are up early! Whatever have you
been doing?"

"Oh, I come up here to pray," she said almost gaily.

"But so do I!"

We stood there together, laughing at what seemed a great
coincidence.

"Come sit down," I said. "I've something to suggest. If you
ever want company, I shall be pleased to have you join me. In bad
weather you'll find me in my office."

Sara looked pleased and not the least bit self-conscious. I found myself drawn to her very closely—and feeling more and more pain over what the future held in store for her.

For some time I had entertained the idea of inviting the girls to early morning prayers in my office or outside depending on the weather Now, while walking back to the school with Sara, I decided that the time had come to set this plan in motion.

An opportunity came several days later during a discussion in my Bible class. The question of prayer was raised. I informed the girls that I always made it a practice to read the Bible and pray each morning before breakfast. "I would be most happy to have any or all of you join me any morning," I added.

And so it began. Sara began coming to my office for morning devotions regularly. Soon other girls joined her. Sara's friendliness and spirit readily attracted the girls to her, and I am sure she played an important part in the steady increase in attendance.

These sessions were most informal. Girls slipped in and out at will. I gave each one a notebook in which to record a daily prayer. Each girl had a special place to keep her notebook in my office.

When a girl wrote down a prayer, she also jotted down the date it was made. As soon as the prayer was answered, this date was also recorded. Sometimes prayers were answered almost immediately. More often it took a long time, and frequently the prayer was such that it might never be answered, at least in a definite way. One of the most important results of this system was that by writing down her prayer, it focused the girl's mind toward the objective—*then she worked hard toward the accomplishment of this prayer.*

In a short time I noticed a new spirit make itself felt in the school. Friendships ripened. Discipline improved. It was amazing what a depth of feeling and friendship could result on a prayer basis.

One day I found an opportunity to talk with Sara alone. For some time I had intended to raise an important point. "Sara," I began, "there is such a thing as studying too much. You should get outside still more, child—and not read quite so much."

"Oh, but I *must* read." Sara spoke with sudden, strong emphasis. Then leaning forward, "You mustn't tell anyone—especially not my mother—but you see, *I'll soon be going blind.* Now is my chance to get all I can—so you see, I must really read and read."

I couldn't trust myself to speak for a moment. "Now come, child. Who gave you that idea?" But my voice sounded hollow to my ears.

"Why the doctor did. I heard him tell mother all about it. But mother must never know that I know. You promise you'll not tell her, won't you?"

"I'll not tell—I promise." Numbed, I wanted to comfort her in my arms. Instead, I merely looked at her helplessly, admiring her wonderful courage and spirit.

"Tell me this," I went on "If what you say is true, how can you feel and act so gay and happy?"

Sara didn't hesitate for an instant. "Aren't we all Christians?" she asked, smiling at me. "Christ knew how He was to be tortured and crucified, but He didn't go around pitying Himself, did He? He improved every hour."

I swallowed hard. "Yes, He improved every hour."

Sara's triumphant spirit touched my heart deeply. All my life I had believed in the power of prayer. At the same time I realized that along with prayer must go hard work plus faith in God's decisions, regardless of how hard it is to understand them at times.

"*Dear God,*" I asked, "*please help this courageous girl who wants to see so badly and who, with sight, could give so much more to the world.*"

Sara and I prayed regularly together, asking for a healing. We remained light-hearted. She continued her intent studying, and I did my best to keep her outside as much as possible.

Months later the eye doctor noticed a sudden change in Sara's eyes. A change for the better. We held our breath. The next examination showed still further improvement.

At the end of three years the "progressive near-sightedness" had completely stopped.

There is a sequel to this story. Sara completed her schooling with a brilliant record. While studying for her doctor's degree at Yale University, she won the Albert Stanburrough Cook Prize for her beautiful religious poem titled "The Return to Eden."

Now, Dr. Sara Deford is assistant professor of English at an eastern college.

PRAYER IS HOW YOU LIVE

by

Herbert H. Harris

As a boy he set out to be tough . . . and he was tough. During World War I Herbert Harris won a battlefield commission and discovered that the real winning combination was one of toughness—with prayer. Mr. Harris, now president of Parfums Charbert, is a nationally prominent perfume manufacturer and producer of the prize-winning play All My Sons.

ALL MY LIFE I'VE BEEN ACUTELY SENSITIVE TO ODORS. ONCE, when I was about five, I was taken to a flower show. They tell me I stood stock still, closed my eyes and breathed in rapture.

"God must smell like that," I said.

It explains exactly how I feel so often—God must smell like that—that's God's fragrance.

My big sister, Rose, brought me up. I was the son of an elderly couple, and when our mother died, Rose, who was already married and a mother, took me in. She and her famous husband, Lew Fields, the great comedian, raised me with their two sons and two daughters. Rose was sister and mother to me, and I don't think it was an easy assignment.

Because I had a marked response to everything beautiful, conversely, I set out to be tough. And I was tough. I was bat boy for the Giants, and no honor or distinction or success I may have

[26]

earned in a lifetime could top the thrill of casual Hi-ya-boy intimacy with such heroes as John McGraw, Christy Mathewson, Roger Bresnahan, Rube Marquard, and Al Bridwell.

That and one other thing sticks out in childhood for sheer triumph. I was a New York City boy from start to finish, and I love New York like monkeys love peanuts. Up on 90th Street is a tree I planted when I was twelve years old. I don't think there's any other tree as beautiful as that one in all the world. It grew along with me, and I visit it regularly. When I'm low or discouraged, I go and commune with that tree and all that Joyce Kilmer felt and meant flows through me. Only God can make a tree, but when I was a kid I helped Him put one in a city. He and I take care of that tree, too.

It's odd the close feeling I had to God from earliest childhood. But I had my own deal with God way back and kept it. The Bible lines which I took as personal guides are: *Not slothful in business; fervent in Spirit; serving the Lord;* and *The greatest of these is Charity.** But this latter has always seemed too easy. There is so much healing, so many untold blessings, and such great returns in giving, that I often wonder where the spiritual benefit is. It's practical as well as thrilling, and where is the nobility in that?

Well, God and I had our understanding, and I steered clear of all religious matters beyond that. I saw so many kinds of religions and they all seem good, but I couldn't understand why it was furiously important that this church or that creed was It. I grew up of Jewish faith, and revere those who truly practice it.

But the day came—as it does, I guess, with every man or woman —when a miracle stopped me short. The word miracle is one of those that makes me uneasy. It affects me like the word "ghost" or "spirits."

It was in France in the first world war. A lieutenant at the time, I was bivouacked in a little village outside of Verdun with eighteen men cut off from everything—news or supplies—while an offensive was launched. The Germans were coming closer and

* *Rom. 12:11 and 1 Cor. 13:13.*

closer; we were between them and the town, and we felt this time
we were goners.

Toward dawn I found in my pocket a letter from my sister Rose,
which I hadn't found time to open. I read it then. My sister
seemed to feel I was in great danger, and she wanted me to know
that her prayers were surrounding me with protection and that
she had others praying for me. I glanced at the others in the room.
They were haggard, scared. They hadn't eaten in twenty-four
hours.

I returned to the letter in which my sister quoted from the
Bible:

> I will say of the Lord, He is my refuge and my fortress; my
> God, in Him will I trust. His truth shall be my shield and
> buckler. Thou shalt not be afraid for the terror by night, nor
> for the arrow that flieth by day; Nor for the pestilence that
> walketh in darkness, nor for the destruction that wasteth at
> noonday.
> A thousand shall fall at thy side, and ten thousand at thy
> right hand, but it shall not come nigh thee.*

I folded the letter and put it inside my shirt. I wasn't fearful any
longer I turned to the men and asked: "Did you see that letter
I was reading? Keep your chin up. Nothing's going to harm us,
because we're being prayed for right this minute. If you guys
here have a prayer in you, I'd suggest you pitch in and help."

One man lying in a corner, spoke up with a big foghorn voice:
"The Lord be with us."

"Amen," I said, for the first time in my life out loud. The whole
roomful repeated it solemnly. I've come to love that word; Amen,
or So be it. It's my favorite prayer.

We had barely finished when the big guns tore loose. The next
five hours were complete indescribable horror, made doubly so
because we were so helpless. I couldn't believe such annihilation
possible, nor such noise or smells. The devil must smell like that.

Not until mid-morning did we realize that the Allies were

* Psalms 91.

busier than the Boche, who started to fall back about that time. I saw the village church crumple like a child's toy, the buildings nearby in smoking ruins. I don't know why I looked at my watch. It was twelve. *Destruction at noonday,* Rose had written. If ever a prophecy was timed that was it. Not one scratch was on any of the nineteen of us there. Nothing in our quarters was disturbed or touched. It was as if a circle had been drawn around our house and barn and the rest of the town wiped out.

Nobody ever again had to convince me of the power of prayer. The mystery is how people can say prayers matter-of-factly, or absent-mindedly It's too potent and dynamic to approach lightly.

While on leave in Paris later, I made my decision to become a perfumer. I'd had quite enough metaphysical wallop through the stenches of war. And I figured out that with five senses we can offend Almighty God with every one except the sense of smell.

Every man at some time likes to think his work is in line with the universe and God's plan. I am convinced that a fragrance can cancel out evil, and can do God's work by inspiring His creatures and appealing to a man or woman's finer qualities, and help them rise above discouragement, melancholy and bitterness. Already some credit is given by psychiatrists to the subtle effects of odors on people. I believe some day we will knowingly use scents to heal and cure. Not all of us are alive to the fact that anger, fear and lust all give off a signal smell, and, conversely, love and generosity and mercy and innocense encase a person in fragrance. We know that horses can smell our fear, that cats can sniff evil in a person. And we all do know that unaired places and unclean things smell —*evil has a stench.*

The churches of old instinctively knew the blessing of odors, the burning of incense, the tang of oils and wax candles, ointment and salt. Of the three gifts brought to the New King by the Wise Men, frank-incense and myrrh were as precious gold.

All these things have a spiritual significance in my work. As for the rest, I live my prayers each day so that I may not fear to meet my Maker at any moment He says my course is run.

WHAT BLOCKS THE
ANSWER TO PRAYER?

by

Clara Beranger

*Which is it with you—"My will be done" or
"Thy will be done"? Ask this question of your-
selves if you wonder why your prayers are not answered. Clara Beranger (Mrs. William C. deMille)
is an instructor of screenwriting at the University
of Southern California and author of the book*
You Can Be Happy.

ABOUT TEN YEARS AGO, I FOUND MYSELF IN A DIFFICULT situation with a problem that seemed unsolvable. I prayed but nothing seemed to happen I was becoming more and more nervous
and unhappy. A friend, who had never talked religion to me,
asked what my trouble was. In despair, I blurted out the story.

"Have you tried prayer?" she asked.

"Yes, but a lot of good that's done me," I answered bitterly.

Quietly she spoke of ways of praying. Without criticizing or
condemning me, she made me see that I was clogging the channel
between me and the Father with negative thoughts, that in all
prayer, it is necessary to have a clean heart and *an open mind.*

."The first step in prayer," she said, "is to let go of what we think
or want and place ourselves and our affairs lovingly in the hands
of the Father. Try that the next time you pray. Let go, get yourself quiet and calm. State your problem to God and then say:
'Dear Father, I leave this to you. I know you will show me the

[30]

right way.' Then *forget your problem*. Believe with all your heart that God hears you and will give you the answer.".

That night I followed her suggestion. I repeated over and over again, "I leave this problem lovingly in the hands of the Father." In the morning, like a flash of light, a solution was shown to me, so simple that I wondered why it had never occurred to me before. I followed the way God led. The situation cleared, and my nervousness and worry disappeared.

Since that time, I have had many occasions to say for myself and for others: "Lovingly in the hands of the Father." And it has never failed me I learned this truth the hard way. Ever since I can remember, I have believed in God, but my times of prayer were irregular, and my method was that of begging for something I particularly wanted.

Many people who have faith in God, and believe theoretically in the power of prayer, wonder sometimes, as I did, why their prayers are not answered as they would like. I think that phrase "as they would like" supplies the answer.

We say *"Thy* will be done," but most of the time we think *"my* will be done." We offer a blueprint of what we want to God, instead of realizing that God sees not only what we want at the moment, but the pattern of our whole life. He knows what is right for us, and His will for us is always good If we believe that with all our mind and heart and mean it when we pray "Thy will be done," we shall receive all that we ask.

Just recently, a dear friend came to me and asked for spiritual help. She is a widow, the only support of herself and her child. Her work, which is highly specialized, has been falling off and she has not been able to make enough for their immediate needs. She said that she has been praying regularly but with no results.

I told her my own experience and repeated what my friend had taught me about prayer. "I will pray with you now. Let us start by saying that we erase all worry and fear for the future, and place your problem lovingly in the hands of the Father. And let us be-

lieve, as we pray, that God is hearing us and that our words will
not return to us void."

We entered the silence together and prayed quietly and silently
for a few moments. Then I said aloud: "Father, we leave this lovingly in Thy hands."

After the prayer we talked for a little while and when my friend
left, she said: "Somehow I feel much better. I believe things will
clear up for me."

Two days later she telephoned and said excitedly that a company for whom she had never worked before called her. She was
starting in with them the next day and they had promised her as
much work as she could handle. "I give thanks to God every minute—and I'll never lose my faith again," she said.

Right after a demonstration, we are *sure* we shall never lose
faith again! But in the pressure of externals, when the world is too
much with us, we are apt to slip back into our old ways of materialistic thinking and living; to forget that spiritual success, like
success in art, athletics or business; means daily discipline. Muscles
grow strong through exercise. So does the soul. God is always
ready for us. Are we always ready for Him?

If you have not been successful in prayer, try taking an honest
mental inventory of your spiritual habits. Do you keep in active
touch with God, or do you just go to Him when you want something? Do you take a few moments out of your busy life *every day*
to read a page or two of the Bible or other inspirational writing, or
to sit quietly and think of God and His blessings you have received? Do you review your day's activities at night to see what
mistakes you may have made, or what good you have accom-
plished?

This nightly review is the best means I know to even the balance between your materialistic and spiritual thought and action.
If you have prayed for good health and continue to be ill, ask yourself if you have been thinking and talking illness. If you have
prayed for prosperity and it has not come to you, find out if you
have been fearing poverty. Success in prayer requires constant af-

firmative thinking, not only when we want some particular thing from God, but when we seem to have all that we need.

In prayer, we have to approach God with clean hands and a pure heart, which I take to mean a mind free from worry and fear, and a heart free from anger, resentment, or hate. Any of these negative emotions blocks the channel between us and God and prevent our good from coming through as it would were the channel free. Jesus said "Ye shall know the truth and the truth shall make you free." Know that God means for us to live abundantly, busily, joyously, free from the ills of body or mind.

Whenever I have prayed with mind and heart clean and pure, with not too definite an outline of how my needs should be met, I have received an answer. And always the answer proved to be for my best good. I could not always see this at the time because what was revealed to me may have differed from what my personal will had dictated. But later I saw that God's will for me was better than my will for myself.

Now I do not outline my will. I put my problem or need lovingly in the hands of the Father and say with perfect sincerity: "Thy will be done. With God all things are possible."

And all things, whatsoever ye shall ask in prayer, believing ye shall receive.

MUCH OBLIGED, DEAR LORD

by

Fulton Oursler

*Fulton Oursler shows how to play an interesting
new game—a game where you can search out every
cause for thankfulness. Mr. Oursler is a senior editor of the* Reader's Digest *and author of the current
radio drama* The Greatest Story Ever Told. *His
latest book is* The Precious Secret.

HER NAME WAS ANNA MARIA CECILY SOPHIA VIRGINIA AVALON
Thessalonians.

She was born into slavery on the Eastern Shore of Maryland
and her earthly master had thought it a great joke to saddle the
little brown baby with that ungainly christening. As a young girl,
in the first year of her freedom, Ann helped the doctor the day my
mother was born That was in 1866. Thirty-seven years later she
was in the bedroom when I was born; she gave me my first bath,
but that was not all she gave me.

I remember her as she sat at the kitchen table in our house; the
hard old brown hands folded across her starched wrapper, the
glistening black eyes lifted to the white-washed ceiling, and the
husky old whispering voice saying:

"Much obliged, dear Lord, for my vittles."

"Ann," I asked, "what is a vittle?"

"It's what I've got to eat and drink—that's vittles."

"But you'd get your vittles whether you thanked the Lord or
not."

"Sure. But it makes everything taste better to be thankful. In some people's religion the whole family does it every meal. But not my church—I do it just for myself."

After the meal was over, she thanked the Lord again and then lit her clay pipe with reedy stem; to this day, every smoking pipe I smell makes me think of my old nurse.

"You know," she said, blowing expert rings in the direction of the kitchen range, "it's a funny thing about being thankful—it's a game an old colored preacher taught me to play. It's looking for things to be thankful for. You don't know how many of them you pass right by, unless you go looking for them.

"Take this morning, for instance. I wake up and I lay there, lazy like, wondering what I got to be thankful for now. And you know what? I can't think of anything. *Tee-hee!* What must the good God think of me, His child, but it's the honest truth—I just can't think of a thing to thank Him for.

"And then, what you think? My daughter, Josie, comes opening the bedroom door and right straight from the kitchen comes the most delicious morning smell that ever tickled my old nose. Coffee! Much obliged, dear Lord, for the coffee and the daughter to have it ready for an old woman when she wakes up. Much obliged, dear Lord, for the smell of it—and for the way it puts ambition even into me. Some people try to tell me coffee is bad, but I've been drinking it for fifty years now and I'm obliged to the dear Lord for every cup I get.

"Now for a while I've got to help Josie with the housework It's a little hard to find anything to thank God for in housework, your ma will tell you the same thing and so will any other woman. But when I come to the mantelpiece to dust the ornaments, there's the Little Boy Blue. How long you think I've had that little China boy? Since before your mother was born. I was a slave when I got it for Christmas. But I never broke it; never even got it chipped. There he sits, all shiny blue, on the mantel, with his golden horn to his mouth. I love that little boy; he's been with me all the time; he's my little mantelpiece brother. Much obliged, dear Lord, for Little Boy Blue.

"And almost everything I touch with the dust rag reminds me of something I love to remember. Even the pictures that hang on the walls. It's like a visit with my folks, here and yonder. Funny, when you get to my age you've got as many of your folks up there as down here. The pictures look at me and I look at them and I remember so much that's good. I get through my housework before I know what I'm doing, I've been so busy remembering.

"You go downtown and look in the windows. So many pretty things."

"But Ann," I broke in. "You can't buy them. You haven't got enough money."

"I've always had enough money for what I want. I don't want those pretty things. What I want a long velvet gown for, trailing halfway behind? But I think it's pretty and I love to stand there and play dolls. Yes, I do. I play dolls in my mind, and I think of your ma, and your Aunt Dot, and your Cousin Leona, how each of them would look in that dress, and I have a lot of fun at that window. I'm much obliged to the dear Lord for playing in my mind, old as I am; it's a kind of happiness.

"Once I got caught in the rain. My daughter Josie thought I would catch my death. *Tee-hee.* It was fun for me. I always heard about fancy people's shower baths. Now I had me one and it was wonderful. So many things are wonderful. That cool water dropping on my cheeks was just exactly like a baby's fingers—and I always loved them.

"You know, God just is giving Heaven away to people all day long. I've been to Druid Hill Park and seen the gardens, but you know what? I likes the old bush in your backyard a sight better. One rose will fill your nose with all the sweetness you can stand. . . ."

Now Ann must have told me these things at different times, but they have ranged themselves in my memory as one long, husky whispered monologue. For a long while I forgot that she had ever said them.

It was not until trouble had clamped down on me with a throttlehold and my old ego had been battered. An hour came when I recognized danger in my own sense of despair. I searched my memory as a bankrupt frantically pokes through safety boxes, looking for a morsel of counsel. Ann had been a long time moldering in her grave, but her rumbling half-whispered tones came back to me, with the game she taught me at the kitchen table of searching out every cause for thankfulness.

I urged myself to play that game . . . I was in the subway at the time, vile-smelling and overcrowded—and it happened there was a burst of laughter that, probably because I was seeking it, reminded me that sorrow passes . . . and I looked about me and marked a young girl's eyes shining with hope for the evening; and again, pride in reading of a batsman's home run bringing glow to the face of a tired old clerk . . . and when I went up on the street, clean snow was falling; a church was lighted and its open doorway called to me. I went in. And I knelt. And my heart filled with warmth when I began to count over my many gifts, my many blessings—how much—how overpoweringly much I had to be grateful for.

For work to be done—good work that I could put my heart into —I'm much obliged, dear Lord, for that. For the ability to take care of those who looked to me. For my loved ones, who love me more than I deserve. For friends; so many who had reached out or spoken, or who had mercifully kept silent in my troubles. And for utter strangers, whom I knew now God had sent to me in my trial, miraculously on hand to help . . . I found the words of thanks tumbling from my lips and heard myself thanking God even for difficulties because they renewed my faith. . . .

There's magic in thanksgiving. You may begin with a cup of coffee, but once you start, the gratefulness swells and the causes multiply. Finally, it seems the more you thank the more you have, and the more you get, to be thankful for—and of course, that's the whole spiritual keystone.

The soul of long-dead Ann was a big soul, big enough to see

God everywhere. I shall never be as big a soul as she was, but she taught me.

The word came from the dingy street where she lived in East Baltimore, with Josie, her daughter, that Ann was dying. I remember mother drove me there in a cab. I stood by Ann's bedside; she was in deep pain and the hard old hands were knotted together in a desperate clutch. Poor old woman, what had she to be thankful for now?

She opened her eyes and looked at us, her eyes lingered with mine.

"Much obliged, dear Lord," she said, "for such fine friends."

She never spoke again—except in my heart. But there she speaks every day. I'm much obliged to God for that.

Your Happiness Formula

YOUR WAY
TO HAPPINESS

by

H. C. Mattern

A personal formula that has worked miracles in the lives of discouraged, beaten individuals is offered here by H. C Mattern. He and his wife, Mary, make a great team. While traveling extensively for business reasons, they both work hard at their avocation—to help people solve their problems and find happiness with God's help.

SOMETIME IN EVERYONE'S EXPERIENCE THE CIRCUMSTANCES OF life seem to gang up on 'em .. one's whole structure just caves in. Life really kicked me solidly in the teeth back in 1930. So much so that I decided that suicide was the only answer.

With my business gone, family ties broken, and eight cents in my pocket, I remember staggering blindly into an open field. The next few moments remain a blurred memory. I was lying on the ground, in agony, when somehow the images of moon and stars penetrated my consciousness.

What then occurred was a deep spiritual experience. I looked into the sky, and every fiber in me went out with a fervid prayer. "God, if you will help me now, ever afterward I will try to help men live again who are down and out."

I suddenly felt reborn. This spiritual experience on top of bitter despair and disillusionment seemed to cleanse my soul. Grateful, I set out to fulfill my promise.

No goal is more intangible than one where you simply try to help other people. After getting my own life on firm footing, I directed my chief efforts toward the down-and-outers; those people who are willing to help themselves, but who need someone to assist them in charting their course.

My greatest asset during these years of building a new life was my continuing faith in God, together with the faith that anyone who will believe in himself can accomplish any goal. Here is an incident, one of many I have experienced, which reveals how such faith in self and God can perform miracles.

One day back in 1946 I was sitting in an office waiting room, thumbing through, for about the thousandth time, the book "Your Key to Happiness." Soon I noticed that the secretary at the desk was gazing intently at the book.

"Are you interested in this book?" I finally asked her with a friendly smile.

She nodded. "Yes, in the title."

"I'll be glad to get you a copy," I replied.

She murmured something about it's being too much trouble. Then, an interruption occurred, and I am sure she forgot the whole conversation.

But I didn't forget it. That night I selected a copy of the book from a supply I keep, marked out several sections, and mailed the book to this secretary, enclosing my personal greeting card. On the back is printed:

"THE WAY TO HAPPINESS"
Keep your heart free from hate, your mind from worry. Live simply; expect little, give much; fill your life with love; scatter sunshine. Forget self. Think of others, and do as you would be done by.
    Try it for a week—you'll be surprised.
                    H. C. Mattern

Some months later I visited this same office again. The sec-

retary, whom I'll call Joan Prescott, recognized me at once. "Please,
Mr. Mattern," she said. "I must see you tonight. I must talk to
you."

I invited her to have dinner with my wife and me, but she
preferred instead to have us both come to her apartment. I noticed
that she was under considerable tension.

When Mary and I arrived at Joan Prescott's apartment, we
had hardly seated ourselves in her small living room before she
was moving about restlessly, flourishing a copy of the book "Your
Key to Happiness."

"What you wrote here in the front of the book . . . do you really
mean that by simply believing hard enough, the impossible can
come true?" she asked with much agitation.

I nodded. What I had written in the front of the book was
simply this: "You can have anything you really desire provided
you believe in God. Write down on paper a description of what
it is that you want, then read over verses 20-27 of the 11th Chapter of Mark. Read them aloud twice a day for ten days. *If you
believe strong enough, the seemingly impossible will come true.*"

Her intent look disturbed me.

"I'm desperate," she admitted. "My marriage is cracking up . . .
Nothing seems to help. . . . My husband is overseas on occupation
duty . . . We only had a few days of marriage before he left. . . .
Now I know he wants to break it off . . .

"If I try your system, and really pray," she continued, "do you
think it will save my marriage—do you think I'd know in a
month's time?"

When I had again given her positive assurance, she thrust a
letter in my hand. "Read this," she directed me almost hysterically.
"Read that part there."

The letter from her husband announced, almost jocularly, that
he had been detailed a special job in Germany that would take
over a year. In a very untactful way he mentioned that his secretary kept him from being too bored with his duties.

"If you will try my plan, and have faith in it, I believe that you and your husband will be reunited—within thirty days." I said, looking her squarely in the eyes.

With this she burst into tears, and my most capable wife then took over the situation. Before we left Joan had agreed to try my faith formula. That night Mary and I both prayed hard for her. As I lay in bed, I found myself saying over the words of verses 20-27 of the 11th Chapter of Mark:

"... I say unto you that whosoever ... shall not doubt in his heart, but shall believe that those things which he saith shall come to pass; he shall have whatsoever he saith."

Thirty days later—to the exact day—Mary and I had a long distance call from Joan Prescott. Her husband had just come home for his discharge—everything was patched up.

"I just can't believe it," she cried. "It's a real miracle ... just like you said it would happen."

Several months later Mary and I had dinner with the reunited couple. With shining eyes they told us the final amazing sequel. Joan's husband had arrived home the night of their wedding anniversary. The next morning they suddenly decided to attend church—the same church in which they had been married.

The minister that Sunday morning preached on the 11th Chapter of Mark. For his text he used verses 20-27.

This plan has worked in equally amazing fashion with many others. It worked with an ex-convict just released from the penitentiary who was afraid he wouldn't be able to make a go of it as a normal citizen. When I found out that he was really sincere, I suggested that he try the formula and place his future in God's hands.

Recently I received a letter from another man who watched this ex-convict's progress. "He is getting along in his own successful way. It is a revelation to me, knowing his past and watching his present."

I met another man who was down and discouraged. "America today offers no opportunities for advancement," he told me. I gave him a copy of "Your Key to Happiness" and recommended the prayer formula. The next time I saw him he was in the ice cream business, brimming with energy and plans for the future.

"Jake," I told him, "you've gotten your feet on the ground. How about paying back God for the opportunities he has given you?"

Jake wanted to know how, so I outlined my idea. "Get acquainted with the postman and obtain from him the names and addresses of poor families with children. Then make it a habit to deliver one quart of ice cream each day to one of these families. Do it yourself, Jake. You could sign the card: 'Jake, The Ice Cream Man.' "

Soon another man discovered the joy that goes with giving as Jake, with sparkling eyes, enthusiastically took up my suggestion.

It is passing onto others what God gives you that is the real "way to happiness." Try it and see for yourself.

HOW EVERYTHING CHANGED FOR THE BETTER

by

Fred Rackliffe

He was a self-admitted failure. Then a remarkable and thorough Christian experience transformed him into a dynamic and successful man. This is the story of Fred Rackliffe, president of Rackliffe Brothers, New Britain, Connecticut, one of the oldest hardware concerns in the state.

CLEM MORTENSON AND I WERE CLOSE FRIENDS AND CLEM WAS concerned about the way I was going. He urged me to attend a meeting at which the missionary E. Stanley Jones was speaking. I didn't know him from Adam. I just went to please Clem. I was so impressed with what he said that I accepted his challenge that this nation was going to go Communist or Fascist unless thinking men went back to the churches and got to work for the Kingdom of God.

I could not wait to call my minister the next morning. When I announced, "I am reporting for duty," he was so flabbergasted he wanted to wait a few days to think it over. I hadn't been going to church at all—couldn't be bothered, just played golf, slept, and read the paper on Sunday morning.

Years before I wanted to be a minister, but my father said to forget it and go into the family hardware business My getting away from church dated from the time I began to drink. After we got married, we had a family and stayed home and took care of them. It wasn't through any error or weakness, we just drifted.

I got started drinking by just being a good fellow. I wasn't a hard drinker, just drank when out with a group, but then when I had one drink I couldn't stop. I never drank alone, but I drank socially. When I drank socially I drank more than I should. I stopped drinking because I made an awful mess of things one night. It broke me all up and I never took another drink.

I am afraid to talk too much about my Christian experience on the theory that I will let my ego into it. The minute you start doing that you begin to think you are quite somebody Perhaps God has used me as an instrument, let's look at it that way. Otherwise I will be taken for an awful sleigh ride some day. As long as Rackliffe remembers where his place is, he will get along all right. I have got to keep my humility and have got to keep it 100%. However, if writing about my experience will help anybody get the great thing that came to me, it will be worth while.

I think from the time I went back into the church on a clean 100% basis and meant what I said, "Not my will but Thine be done," and tried to live the life I should live, from that time on everything checked to my success. Everything flowed toward me instead of away from me. I enjoyed happiness I hadn't enjoyed for years. I was released. The minute I turned from the things I had been doing (it wasn't the Christian life I was living), the minute I started to put my mind on God and on God's will, many things cleared up right away.

"You can't make an error of judgment if you are 100% with God," says J. C. Penney. Things dissipate if you are not living the right way.

I had a terrific temper before. My wife says that I am different to live with now. I feel a sense of control I didn't have before.

You cannot be a percentage Christian. If you think for one minute you can be 86% Christian and 14% unChristian, the 14%

will cause your downfall. You can't make a deal with God. You are either all-Christian or not-Christian, if you want to be successful. You cannot compromise.

When I reported back to the minister, the first job he gave me was to take charge of the discussion at "The People's Fifteen Minutes" at church every Thursday night. That assignment made me stand up and tell the whole gang why I was back in church. Then, in order to have the proper discussions on the assigned topics, I had to go to see a few people each week before the meeting and ask them to help me out in the discussion. In that way I got to know people and realized that there were a fine lot of people in the church. I asked them to say something on their favorite scripture passage in the meeting so that I wouldn't be talking the entire fifteen minutes. In this way I got them to talk. I planted people in the audience to start discussions.

The young people's group was weak, only six youngsters. The minister said, "That is your baby, develop it." I applied business methods to build up the class. I wrote sales letters to them and got them interested. Then I admonished them, "I don't want you here if your father or mother sends you. If you are interested in studying with me, you can come; but if you aren't interested and just come because your mother sends you, I don't want you. I don't want anybody to be a member of the class who doesn't want to come of his own accord." Every Sunday afternoon I call all those who weren't present that morning. I ask them if they don't like what I am saying, or if they have lost interest, and if so, don't they think they should send me a resignation.

They wanted me to talk to them. This was hard for me to do at first because I wasn't used to it. In doing this I discovered that all the things good for a high school age person are good for a man of my age, as for example, living Christianity instead of talking about it so much.

Because I have come back into the church and become active, I do not make any member of my family do what I did, but I try to set the example for them in daily life. Then it is up to them. I am not trying to jam it down their throats.

Perhaps my experience with resentment is the biggest thing in my new life. I used to make myself miserable with resentment and ill-will. I read, "Vengeance is mine, I will repay, saith the Lord." That gave me the idea that "getting even" is God's business. If you take the same amount of thinking and planning that you have been putting on resentment and getting even with somebody and put it on the positive side, you will really get somewhere. I pass it over to the Lord, and it relieves me no end. Resentment passes and inner peace comes. It is wonderful to be able to look at somebody else and enjoy with him his success without saying enviously, "Why is he entitled to that?" Now I can get a lot of real joy out of other people's success. I enjoy it; bask in it. I used to hate it, I used to get sun-burned in it.

I don't claim to be a saint. I have times when I would like to throw the whole thing out the window and forget it. Such is human frailty, but every time I feel that way new strength is given me.

The ability to take criticism and grow under it is the mark of a man. I used to bridle up. My pride made me touchy. My secretary did me the most good. One day she said, "Don't you know that we all know you are the president of this company?" I stopped to think a minute and then laughed and said, "Why, have I been trying to impress you?" She said, "And how!" Ever since she said that, I have tried to develop a real humility without being "milk toast."

I find help in getting together with a group of business men every Tuesday noon—a few business man and the minister. We read passages of scripture, meditate, and then have lunch together. We have ten minutes of absolute silence. A room can become spiritually charged with a few men sitting around and not saying anything for ten minutes.

Christianity isn't just a Sunday exercise. It is an every-day-of-the-week proposition. I enjoy going to church because the type of sermons I hear in our church are down-to-earth, real, vital, every-day stuff. They send me out with a spring in my step. Christianity works. It has made everything different. I have found my answer.

I WAS MISSING
SOMETHING

by

John J. Porter

A church-goer for years discovers to his amazement that what he had been hearing Sunday after Sunday really works Jagged nerves were calmed, fears overcome and inner peace secured. John J. Porter, Chairman of the Board of the North American Cement Corporation, was then prompted to declare, "I was missing something!"

FOR MANY YEARS MY RELIGION MEANT VERY LITTLE TO ME. I was a nominal Christian, with "enough Christianity to be decent, but not enough to be dynamic."

In middle age I was led by a combination of circumstances to attend a church where I heard preached week after week the application of religion to personal living. I heard of the marvelous things that Christ can do for those who accept Him wholeheartedly . . . how nerves can be quieted, irritability and bad temper controlled, fear and apprehension abolished and poise and inner peace secured. I came to realize what I was missing and I wanted these things.

After a long argument with myself, it finally became clear that what was standing in my way were certain ambitions, not wrong in themselves, but wrong only in that I had made them the main objectives in my life.

From a New England ancestry I inherited a taste for thrift, an

[51]

intense desire for financial security and a pride in achieving this by my own efforts. In my latter years I had also developed a desire for leisure time for certain hobbies and a selfish impatience with any activities which might interfere with them It became clear to me now that as long as I put these things *first* I was denying to Christ what I owed him.

It was hard to do but I finally made the decision and told God that all that I had was His to do with as He chose, that His will would be my sole objective. The immediate result was a sense of relief and of peace such as I had never had before. Other results came gradually over a period of ten years, during which time there have been three phases in my spiritual development.

It took time to become accustomed to the idea of putting God first, to acquire the habit of asking His guidance and to learn how to recognize His answers. Because I realized the importance of these things I worked hard at them and, while I have acquired with practice certain skills, I expect to continue to work at them during the rest of my life.

My greatest difficulty at first was to be sure of His will. I have tried very hard to get direct messages and I have had a very few wonderful experiences; but I realize now that God prefers to speak to us through our intellect, our conscience and His words when on earth, as recorded in the Bible. I know that He will direct and guide my thoughts if I ask Him and I have convincing proofs of this. For example, it has often happened that when I start to prepare a Bible Class lesson my mind is utterly barren of ideas; but if I lay aside my books and ask God to give me a plan for the development of the lesson He never fails to respond. Usually the ideas come so promptly as to seem miraculous.

One of my difficulties has always been bad temper and a tendency to become irritated easily at bad manners and lack of consideration for others, such as, for example, smoking in a crowded elevator, or unnecessary pushing in the subway. There was a time when such an incident would "burn me up inside" I had to learn a technique for overcoming this, and my practice now is to try to remember that the offender does not know any better and that he may be a very good man in other respects. I make a silent prayer that God may bless him and show him the light. The result to me is a glow of satisfaction rather than the burn of anger.

It is hard to overcome the bad habits of a lifetime, but I have made some progress and I believe that my wife and my associates would testify that I am at least easier to live with.

I have learned not to be afraid of any assignment that conscience tells me I should accept. I have found by experience that, providing I have no motive of personal pride and look at it solely as an opportunity to serve God, He will see me through.

I have also found that while these assignments take much time, in fact at times seem rather overwhelming, they carry their own reward in pleasure.

Financially, my covenant with God has worked out in this way. My wife and I are now giving five times the proportion of our income; but this did not come all at once Perhaps He did not wish to try me too greatly at first, but at any rate I have had very clear messages as to what I should do. I know that He wants me to handle as a trustee the money He has permitted me to make and that He expects me to try to use it to the very best advantage in His work. I have an idea that as time goes on He will ask and make it possible for us to give more and more.

God has certainly prospered me financially and many times I have direct guidance from Him. On one occasion particularly I was confronted with a personal business problem involving, for me, a considerable sum of money. I analyzed the proposition forward and backward, but was unable to make up my mind. Finally I did what I should have done in the first place—ask God for His advice. So promptly that it seemed miraculous, the pieces of the puzzle fell into place and the answer came to me to go ahead. The result is not less interesting.

The original purpose of the transaction has not yet worked out (although it may still do so), but the value of my purchase has multiplied several times and promises to be exceedingly profitable.

Truly the ways of God are beyond our understanding, and I have learned from this and other instances not to ask for specific results, but only that He may guide my thoughts to the end that everything may work out for the best. If in His wisdom it appears that financial success is not best for me, I shall try to accept that too.

To sum up—I have gotten from the decision to give myself unreservedly to God and for the work done to make this decision effective, the following.

First: Security in the knowledge that He will take care of my material needs.

Second: Happiness through the realization that self is not important.

Third: Inner peace from the lifting of fear and concern for what may happen in the future.

MY FORMULA FOR
VICTORIOUS LIVING

by

John G. Ramsey

*"Mother is boss in our home," the neighbor's
daughter said once to John Ramsey's young son.
"Who's boss in yours?" "God is boss in our home,"
young Ramsey answered. This is the key to the triumphant formula used so successfully by Mr.
Ramsey, both in his home life and as public relations representative of the United Steel Workers
of America (C.I.O.).*

SOME TIME AGO I SAT DOWN AT A TABLE FOR FOUR IN A DINING
car. Three other men were already seated; as I later discovered,
none was acquainted with the other. They all seemed gloomy and
depressed. As I do not like to eat a meal in such an atmosphere,
I began a conversation which I hoped would lift their spirits. Soon
we were talking animatedly—mostly about religion.

After we finished dinner, one said to me, "I'd like to talk with
you for a few moments"

"Certainly," I replied, "let's go into the lounge car"

The Lord must have wanted this conversation to be held, for
even though the train was crowded two seats, side by side, awaited
us. My new companion told me that when he left home as a boy,
his father enjoined him never to allow more than ten minutes to
elapse upon a train before talking to the nearest person about his
religious life.

"On my first train ride," he said, "I was seated next to a burly fellow. I kept my eye upon my watch until ten minutes had passed; then, scared to death, I blurted out, 'Are you saved?' I got the rough answer you might expect, and for twenty years I have never spoken to another man about religion

"Today," he continued, "you got three men, none of whom had met the other, talking about religion naturally and interestingly in a couple of minutes. What's your technique?"

We chatted for some time and, as he arose to leave, he introduced himself as vice president of a certain steel company; then he asked me my name and business.

"I am John Ramsey," I replied. "I'm an organizer for the United Steel Workers of America, and it is my job to organize employees of your company."

Despite differences in point of view, we established fellowship and understanding based upon our common religious faith. I have never thought much about my "technique," except that it is to try to live a God-centered life. I was a steel worker for seventeen years, performing manual labor. During the depression, when I went through some difficult circumstances, I attended a religious meeting on a Pennsylvania mountain top. The world was so beautiful that morning that it seemed a great inconsistency for sin and ugliness to exist. I decided to dedicate my life to bringing beauty to everyone, and, to my way of thinking, this also meant raising the economic standard everywhere.

I have no cut-and-dried program. I ask God for guidance in everything I do. This, I find, releases a power that helps amazingly in even the smallest matters; and it certainly is a help in the bigger issues.

My son Dicky taught me a lot. We have in our home a family "quiet time." At the end of it we share what thoughts God gave us during our meditation One day, Dicky said at the end of a "quiet time," that he had a message. "If there is the tiniest bit of wrong, stop right away and ask God what to do about it."

In the years that followed, that guidance of a little four-year-old boy has been a constant challenge to me.

Once I was a witness for nine consecutive days in a National Labor Relations Board case. Seven of those days were cross-examination. After that length of time on the stand, one would be nervous; yet, by praying to and feeling the presence of God, I continued with clear mind and unruffled feelings. At one time the corporation counsel asked me, "Are you afraid of the company?"

"No," I answered.

Counsel continued: "Do you consider yourself different from other men? If so, please explain to the court."

"Yes," I said. "The men I work with put their faith of security into the hands of the company. My wife and I have put our faith of security into the hands of God."

During the cross-examination the company counsel gave me a leading question. The question was to the effect of whether I was employed by a company or a corporation. I realized my answer was very important. Due to a legal technicality in the phrasing of the question I had to leave the court room before answering. When in the hall I asked God to give me the correct answer to the question. He told me to look on my pay stub, and there I found printed, "Subsidiary Companies of the Corporation." When I resumed the stand my answer astonished the counsel of the company and the Labor Board.

That is the way God works when you put your trust completely in Him. I need to have meditation with God. The Lord can tell me so much in two minutes that I must go out and get busy. Often I need to stop and pray. In the busiest hours of the day I feel the need of constant communion with God.

I try to make my spiritual experience natural. I like to wake up naturally in the morning, feeling that the Lord is waiting to speak to me. When an alarm clock awakens me, however, it doesn't seem a natural awakening.

We practice in our family the principle of a God-centered life. One night we were having a dinner of left-overs, and there was one piece of cherry pie which happened to be at Billy's place. Johnny saw the pie and wanted it. Had we been on the old basis of non-spiritual living, I would have become angry and thrown the pie into the garbage can; and nobody would have had it. However, Mother said, "Let's be quiet and see what God wants us to do about this pie. If we eat dinner under this tension, we're likely to get ulcers of the stomach."

That was a sensible attitude, so we had a quiet talk with God regarding the pie. The first to share his thoughts was Billy, who said that he should be unselfish and that Johnny could have the pie. Johnny said that under such circumstances Billy would be happy while he would not. Therefore, Billy ate the pie, all were happy, and there were no stomach ulcers. If God can settle conflicts within an individual and conflicts within a family, He can also help to settle conflicts among groups in society. The whole question is who is the director of your life.

One day a neighbor's boy told my son about an argument his father and mother staged the night before. He said, "Mother is boss in our home. Who is boss in your home—your father or your mother?"

With hardly a moment for thought, my son said, "God is boss in our home."

WHAT'S SO DIFFICULT
ABOUT FAITH?

by

H. I. Phillips

Every reader of the New York Sun *gets a
chuckle and an inspiration from H I. Phillips,
famed columnist. He makes faith seem so reasonable because he's proved it to be so in his own experience*

HAVE YOU NOTICED THAT MAN WHO, REFUSING TO ACCEPT CER-
tain religious concepts on the ground that he doesn't understand
them completely, seldom has the remotest idea what makes his
windshield wiper work?

Have you observed that the fellow who argues "But I can't accept anything so baffling to my intelligence," has the fullest faith
in his radio or his telephone, without anything beyond a sketchy
idea how they do what they do?

Whenever I get into one of those moods when I feel any doubt
about anything in the Bible I switch myself back onto the track of
faith by realizing that no story in it is harder for my mind to com-
prehend than hundreds of wonders which I accept in everyday
life as routine.

I don't say when I hear in a Bronx flat a voice from Teheran
or Mandalay that it is too incredible to believe. When I sit in a
Connecticut bungalow and a crooner out in Los Angeles comes
right into my room with me by airwave I never think of saying
"That's too much for me to swallow."

Why should miracles of Holy Writ seem hard to take when one

realizes they were performed by a Man compared to Whom we are intellectual pygmies? Nobody contends that Marconi, Bell, Edison, and Morse were smarter than God.

So, out with the shabby alibi of believing only in what you clearly understand! You take countless things in your routine life entirely on faith, and you couldn't give a comprehensible explanation of how any of them work.

Nothing the church teaches could strike me as difficult to accept after, in my hotel room in Miami, Florida, I have seen and heard by airwaves my Aunt Minnie in Wappingers Falls, N. Y.

In fact, the experience with Aunt Minnie makes it easier.

I used to wonder about and question some of the amazing things about the religion taught me at my mother's knee, but that was back in a somewhat less amazing era. I can't see how children of today, accustomed to incredible feats of science all about them, can find any Bible story puzzling.

I think the past war has restored prayer to its old-fashioned place in life. Certainly more people in more places have been praying with more vigor than ever before.

I believe in prayer unquestioningly. But I think more emphasis is needed in the churches and in the homes on the quality and mood and spirit of prayer. There might well be some national "Week for Careful and Intensive Praying," as against the all too common hurried, mumbled superficial prayer.

Of all things that should not be slipshod, fumbling and hasty, except in an emergency, is a talk with God. We all seem to have plenty of time for other things of life. No man goes into a business conference without plenty of careful thought about what he is going to say. If a fellow expects to be called on for a few remarks at a dinner he generally worries about it for days in advance. What makes us think that in the matter of prayer we can take out a few minutes a day for a sort of "quicky," often poorly thought out and poorly executed?

The most vital talks of your life are the ones you hold with your Creator. And that is the one time you are communing with One who isn't fooled or imposed upon.

I think of the radio again in connection with prayer, and it seems to me that to reach God, one has to tune in properly just as it is necessary to tune in to get anybody on the radio. We will fuss with a radio any length of time in order to get the right reception and we know the tuning has to be perfect "How come" a man can assume that he can get in touch with God fully and completely by any swift, hit-or-miss routine which is characterized chiefly by lack of preparation, deep thought or a perfect "tuning-in?"

Try as we may, we may not be able to get tuned in with God properly, but we certainly should make the effort with patience, intensity, and care.

Prayer is the most solemn and most important act of daily life. It rates over all else It is a "must," as they say in the business world. And while we should do it often in a spirit of worship and gratitude and without asking or imploring special attention or favors, it is comforting to feel that we are praying in a way that might make an answer possible, and not in a manner that would almost be an insult if talking over a telephone.

I would like to hear more said in the churches about preparation for prayer, about the dignity of it and the need for care and concentration, with no regard for the fleeing minutes.

I would like to see the casual, hasty, routine type of prayer frowned upon.

I don't think one can talk with God without infinitely more reverence, patience, concentration and thought than one shows when talking to a neighbor. And I know most of my neighbors wouldn't even notice me if I were as casual, abrupt and hurried in what I had to say to them as I sometimes am in presuming to say something to my Maker.

P.S.—Of course it makes a difference, I guess, who's praying. Probably a man or woman whose life has been lived close to God and in keeping with his teachings is listened to more fully and understandingly, even when he or she prays in a hurry, than I am when I pray with all the time and patience at my command. Did I say "probably?" I mean "certainly."

Finding the Success Spark

HUMAN RELATIONS
AND BUSINESS SUCCESS

by

A. O. Malmberg

In three months the worst salesman in the company becomes the best! Proper leadership inspired this remarkable reversal. Mr. A. O. Malmberg, director of public relations of the Doughnut Corporation of America and nationally known leader of management conferences, points out the sensible tie-up of religious principles with practical business procedures.

YEARS AGO I WAS A TYPICAL SALES MANAGER IN A LARGE EASTERN company employing 888 salesmen. I drove the men hard, worked long hours, coined snappy slogans, but something was definitely wrong. I was getting nowhere, and what was worse couldn't put my finger on the trouble. I felt like I was plunging my fist into a ton of Jello.

The company was doing fine. The president appeared highly pleased at rising sales trends, but in my heart I knew that I was failing. We would have big sales campaigns, business would soar, salesmen would get their bonuses, then sales would drop back to pre-campaign levels. It was exasperating. The men seemed to produce only what was called for. No more.

A sense of failure began to weigh me down. The company president was pleased because he measured sales performance against past records; but I was dissatisfied because I knew that our salesmen could do better if they only would.

[65]

Convinced that something was fundamentally wrong, I moved to Denver and took a position as sales manager in the same industry. Instead of 888 salesmen, I now had 28 under my supervision. A period of trial, error and human analysis loomed ahead, but I welcomed it as a laboratory in which I could experiment to find how to change human *won't* power to *will* power.

For long hours I pondered over the operation of those two powerful spiritual intangibles in business—loyalty and co-operation. I had obtained neither. Why? Because I drove the men too hard? Possibly. Deep down though I knew that wasn't the only reason. I had failed to reach the dynamic will to work of the men under me; I had not inspired loyalty and co-operation.

My thinking revolved around the one question how to get salesmen to *want* to work? Experience had taught me that men will not put their hearts into a job if they dislike, or have no respect for, their boss. Gradually the conviction developed that to achieve better human leadership, I should pattern my management methods after those used by the greatest leader and salesman of them all—the Master himself. Christian principles in daily action—in modern business. Once planted in my mind, the idea grew like a snowball rolling down hill.

First, I arrived at a new definition of business—business not as the management of things, but the development of people. Always the accent on *people*. Better people, better business—the two were hand in glove.

When I commenced work on this new job, one of our employees, whom we will call Charlie Cox, immediately attracted my attention. He was so inept, so careless on his route that he hardly ranked as a salesman at all. Around the company he was a target for jokes, a butt for pranks, all of which he took good-naturedly. But that wasn't what really interested me. Cox loved animals, and they got the attention his route should have received.

A friend of every cat and dog in the neighborhood, Cox stopped at butcher shops each morning and filled an old sack with bones and meat scraps. Then as he made his rounds, he doled out his supply of scraps to his animal friends. Housewives and people along the way tagged him as a "character," but they always had a cheery word for him, and Charlie for them. For Charlie also loved people.

This wistful charm undoubtedly kept Cox on the payroll, for his record certainly warranted a dismissal. I did some deep thinking Here was a grand opportunity to practice new man-development methods. Lincoln's famous saying, the fundamental of all selling, came to mind "If you would win a man to your cause, first convince him that you are his friend."

One day I dropped in on Cox just after he had finished his route. He was dusty, tired I pretended that mine was just a casual call. "Cox, how goes it?" I asked.

Cox smiled wearily. "Just fine . . . except I haven't any new business to report."

"Tell me, Cox, do you like your work?" I continued.

"Oh, yes," he said, brightening up. "I've always liked being a salesman because I meet so many people and . . ." He didn't finish, but I knew he was thinking of his animal friends.

"Are you satisfied with the money you are making?"

A slight shadow clouded Cox's face He began to fidget in his chair. "Well, not quite. My wife has a bad eye She needs an operation, and I can't make enough money to pay for it."

Here was an opening With a friendly gesture I placed my hand on his shoulder. "Cox, listen to me. You are a born salesman. Do you know why? Because you love animals, because you love people. You could be the best salesman in our company if you wanted to be. You could make enough money to pay for ten operations if you really wanted to. And always remember—you are very important to our company and we need your help."

Cox sat quietly, a pensive look in his eyes. I felt a great compassion for this man. Had I said the right thing? Now Cox was fumbling in his vest pocket. He pulled out his watch, opened the back side, gazed at it for a moment, then handed it to me. Inscribed were these words: "To Charles Cox—winner of first prize in the national sales contest of the Hoover Vacuum Cleaner Company—year 19—."

This was an unexpected twist. Cox had really been a top-flight salesman. I stared at the inscription, visualizing the story it told. Cox riding the crest of success, then a few tough breaks . . . sensitive feelings bruised, perhaps poorly handled by the sales manager . . . the beginning of lost confidence . . . the competitive spark dying . . . the inevitable road down.

Suddenly I felt a tremendous lift. Here sat a man with tear-filled eyes, moved—all because I had given him a friendly pat on the back. Starved for small crumbs of praise, grateful because I had told him that he was important, Cox was feeling old sensations stirring inside. The embers of long-banked, competitive fires were being rekindled. A new light shone out of his blurred eyes. I glowed with a greater sense of accomplishment than if I had made the sale of the year, for I *had penetrated to the source of power within this man.*

The next day when Cox arrived at the plant, his fellow salesmen looked at him in amazement. He had a mirror finish to his shoes, his clothes were pressed, a handkerchief perched jauntily in his coat pocket. With quiet determination he approached my desk. "Today I make a new start," he said. "We'll show these fellows around here a brand of salesmanship they've never seen before."

Cox's transformation did something to every member of the company. He soon set a pace that had the other salesmen gasping and redoubling their efforts to keep up. This spirit penetrated every department of the company. Within three months Cox soared from last place to top position among the salesmen. He earned enough money in commissions and bonuses to give his wife the sorely needed eye operation. He vindicated himself in his own eyes and before his fellow workers.

It took the Cox experience to start my thinking along the lines of better human leadership. As more responsible jobs and more involved problems came my way, I had further opportunities to use Christian principles in dealing with men, in easing industrial tension. My "trial and error" system proved to me that only better men build better business.

William Holman Hunt, great English artist of the pre-Raphaelite school, painted a beautiful garden scene which was hung in the Royal Art Gallery in London. The painting so appropriately called "The Light of the World" shows the Master standing in the garden at midnight, holding a lantern and leaning toward a heavily paneled door. He was knocking on the door and awaiting an answer from within.

A critic looked at the painting, turned to Mr. Hunt and said: "Lovely painting, Mr. Hunt, but you've forgotten something. That door upon which the Master is knocking ... is it never to be opened? You've forgotten to put a handle on the door."

Then Mr. Hunt smiled with great understanding. "My friend, that door on which the Master is knocking is not just an ordinary door. *It is the door to the human heart. It needs no handle for it can only be opened from within.*"

Small wonder that Mr. Hunt was a master artist. He had *insight* and *understanding*—two indispensable qualities of great leaders of men. The critic only had eyesight and knowledge, so he understood not. Until leaders of men develop *insight* and *understanding* there will be little industrial peace.

It takes a spiritually sensitive leadership to reach through to the emotional power within the individual Only in this way can we eliminate *won't* power and release *will* power.

FINDING THE HIDDEN
SUCCESS SPARK

by

John Glossinger

A shipping clerk who never earned more than $35 per week in sixteen years with his firm suddenly capitalizes on hidden abilities and soon is making $10,000 a year. What happened? John Glossinger, retired president of the Kny-Scheerer Corporation, and author of the volume You Are Born To Victory, *shows how a person can find himself and master the secret of personal victory.*

A BOY IN OUR WAREHOUSE PACKING DEPARTMENT WAS DOING well, for he had the two ingredients for advancement—integrity and energy. Complimenting him on his work, I said, "You are a fine packer, but you must not be content with merely being a shipping clerk."

"Oh," said the boy, "I haven't got the stuff to get ahead. I can do this job. I'm satisfied. Besides, I make too many mistakes to go very far."

"If you set your goal high enough," I told him, "you can become president of this company."

I put a picture in his mind of himself as president of the company, for one tends to become what he honestly thinks himself capable of being.

Oftentimes people are afraid to make mistakes. Nobody ever got anywhere who was afraid to make a mistake. When I place a man in an important job, I give him a send-off along this line:

"I am putting you in a position of responsibility. You are going to make mistakes. Go ahead and work hard and don't be afraid to make them. I'll underwrite your mistakes. A man who is afraid to make a mistake will never have the courage to make an effort."

During my thirty-eight years in business I have received many real thrills from my work in helping people to develop their own abilities.

One outstanding fact impressed me above all others—that a great, if not the greatest, asset in a business organization is the hidden power inherent in the men and women who compose it. The big job in bringing out this hidden potential is to crack shells—shells for fear, timidity, or inferiority.

A thirty-two-year-old man, whom we will call Frank, proved to be one of the most unapproachable men I ever tried to arouse to achievement. He had been with the company for sixteen years as a clerk. At the end of this time he was making thirty-five dollars a week.

Shy, unresponsive, glum, he never spoke to anyone unless spoken to. At quitting time he would vanish without even a good-bye. He could never be persuaded to attend Christmas parties or any other social affairs among his fellow workers. He seemed afraid of himself, of the world and all the people in it.

I was impressed by several of his qualities. He had integrity and he did his job conscientiously. One day, I called him into my office. Ill-at-ease, nervous, Frank sat down by my desk.

"Frank," I said, "you have the qualities to get ahead in this business. I'd like to help you make something of yourself."

He looked at me quickly as much as to say: "What's your angle, brother? Why pick on me?"

"Let's face it," I continued. "You've been doing the same kind of work for sixteen years at about the same salary. You're in a rut. I want to help you work up to a more responsible job."

Frank was stiff and unbending. At the mention of salary, I

could sense his unspoken thought, "It's your fault for not paying me more."

Since Frank was so shy and suspicious of my interest in him, I knew a series of talks would be necessary to loosen him up. Then, after several such discussions came an admission.

"Mr. Glossinger," he said, "it's just no use. I never had enough education to make anything of myself."

So this was the cause of his feeling of inferiority!

Little by little I managed to piece out his story. Not only did he feel that his lack of education was too big a handicap, but his father had been a failure also. Like father, like son, he figured. With no money, no influence, no contacts, and no education, how was he ever to get anywhere?

But I kept hammering at the shell around him, trying to get him to open up more about the office, to work toward a better job, to think success. Soon though I began to wonder if he wasn't too tough a nut to crack. Then one day he sat in my office and expressed complete lack of confidence in what I was trying to do. "Let's call it quits," he muttered unhappily.

Frank was discouraged and glum. I was baffled. It was a hot day and the heat in my office was most oppressive. Frank's collar was open and then I noticed a gold chain around his neck.

At the end of the chain was a cross.

"Frank," I said, suddenly struck with an idea. "Whenever I am in deep trouble or have a problem I cannot solve, I always go to a Higher Power for help. I have never failed to get help when I do this. Now I want to make you a proposition."

A faint sign of interest cracked Frank's expressionless face.

"Tonight before you go to bed I want you to pray for the answer to the problem we've been trying to work out. You and I will both pray to Almighty God for His help."

Frank's face lit up with real understanding. This was something in line with his strong religious training. The idea of taking his problems to God appealed to him. I had finally struck a responsive chord in this man—through his religion.

During the next few weeks I made it a point to watch Frank fairly closely. There were signs of improvement. Little things. He was more friendly to his fellow employees. He was making a definite effort to shake off his lethargy.

Then one day he came to work with a box in his hand. Self-consciously, he entered the main office of typists, clerks and secretaries, then took off the wrapping—*around a box of candy*. Nervously he placed the box on a central table with an attempt at casualness Hardly any of the employees had even noticed him.

"Here's some candy for anyone who wants it."

He said it so inaudibly that almost no one heard him. But one typist did. "Why, Frank," she said. "Is this for us? How nice!"

Heads popped up all over the room. They looked at Frank in amazement. Frank, his face a bright crimson, hastily retreated to his desk and busied himself with some papers to hide his embarrassment. An unobserved spectator to this little scene, I felt a warm glow the rest of the day.

During the next weeks Frank continued to expand his personality. He talked more fluently with me. He began to say "Good mornings" and "Good nights" to his fellow workers. Again little things. But like the box of candy, they all added up.

Then one day I called him in to tell him we were ready for the next step. "Frank, we are going to make a salesman out of you. You're going out on the road."

At this he grew very pale. "Oh, no. I could never do that. I can talk to you now—but not to strangers."

I stopped him short. "We've started something, Frank. You can't turn back now. You have got to go on."

Then I called in one of my salesmen and explained to him that he was to take Frank with him on his next trip. Frank was to learn how to approach customers, how to talk to them and how to sell our products.

Their trip took them through New England, New York and Pennsylvania. Finally, there was just one more city left—Wheeling, West Virginia. According to my pre-arranged instructions, the salesman broke the news to Frank in Pittsburgh.

"Frank," he said, "you will have to cover Wheeling yourself. You know the routine well enough now. I've got to go back to New York today."

Frank later confessed to me that when the salesman left him, his world suddenly collapsed around him. "There I was, four hundred miles from home, all alone," he said. "I was scared stiff. Then I remembered your suggestion that whenever there was a tough problem to solve, you consulted a Higher Power. I had done this before, and it had helped me. I did it then. The next morning I went on to Wheeling."

To Frank's surprise the customers received him kindly and graciously. He ended up with several fine orders. When he walked out of the last establishment, the old shell around him fell off completely.

It isn't necessary to add that today Frank is in the ten thousand dollar a year income bracket.

In every man there is some unknown spark which, if ignited, can transform a failure into a success. With Frank it was his religion. I am sure many others can be reached the same way. The potentials are in every person, provided he or she has integrity and energy.

THEY CALL ME
"SUCCESS STORY"

by

Lane Bryant

*The faith of our fathers is strong within us . . .
and the influence of our grandparents helps us in
moments of distress and decision. Lane Bryant,
immigrant girl at sixteen, now has a great Fifth
Avenue store bearing her name, and a four-acre
mail-order plant in Indianapolis fills over 10,-
000 orders a day Begun on a needle and thread
basis, the Lane Bryant sales now are in the fifty
million dollars a year bracket.*

I WAS BORN LENA HIMMELSTEIN IN A SMALL VILLAGE IN LITHU-
ania and my mother died when I was ten days old. My older
sister and I were brought up by our grandparents. For generations
all the men in my family had been rabbis, educated but poor. In
my childhood, Jews were not allowed to go to Czarist schools but
my grandfather taught me reading, writing and arithmetic, and
knowledge far more important.

Always his firm rich voice lived with me, instructing me: "Any
work that helps another human being has dignity. The only real
success comes from filling a human need." And in desperate
times, his tones would echo in memory, with the words of the
Talmud: "Forget not your God."

My sister migrated to the United States early, and when I was
sixteen years old, some distant relatives offered to take me in

1897. Arriving at Castle Gardens, New York, we were met by a young man who greeted me exuberantly—as his bride! These relatives of mine had promised to bring their son a wife of his own people, hard-working and young—but they had neglected to tell *me!* I'm afraid I shocked them all with my indignant refusal, as I stalked off.

My sister was a seamstress in a shop, and there I was hired for one dollar a week. As I worked, learning English and the use of that fabulous wonder, the sewing machine, I was ecstatic over the loveliness of delicate negligees and sumptuous underwear, laces, ribbons, and embroideries. Soon I found another job, as a first class machine operator at four dollars a week more. I met, and within a year married David Bryant, a jeweler, older than I, and in my eyes a sophisticated man of the world. Ten months later our son Raphael was born, and within a year my husband, David Bryant, had died.

As I hugged my infant son to me, lonely and worried, I felt I could hear my grandfather's voice repeating: "Remember me, O my God, and wipe out not my good deeds that I have done for the house of my God."

The wedding gift from my husband of a pair of diamond earrings was often pawned to pay on a sewing machine—or rent. With a baby, I could not go out to work, but I could do piece work at home and live with my sister. So I started an on-the-premises business of fine bridal lingerie.

These I delivered personally, sometimes waiting hours to be paid. Money was necessary to buy material to make more.

In a few years, I opened a real shop on the first floor of a five-story building on Fifth Avenue and 120th Street. Nearby was Mt. Morris Park with grass and trees and a place to air the baby. There was a five dollar petticoat in the window, and in the back I worked at my machine, often with my baby on my lap—the child that was to grow up to be president of the business! My trade grew entirely from the fact that one customer would recommend me to another.

In 1907 I borrowed $300 from my brother-in-law to open a bank account. Now there would be a real shop separate from our living quarters. But the bank so awed me, the papers and whole procedure so rattled me that I signed my name L-A-N-E instead of L E N A, and then was too embarrassed to try to explain. From that day on, I was Lane Bryant.

My work began to be known at an astonishing rate. All the customers, as they married and expected babies, needed many negligees, for in those days women kept to the house in pregnancy. But my fate was decided when an expectant mother tearfully pleaded:

"I want so terribly to entertain at home. Couldn't you design a gown to hide my condition?"

That problem challenged me—and I found that by inserting an elastic in the waist band of a silk sun-pleated skirt, the customer could wear it without provoking comment. Soon others clamored for the same service of disguise, and there I was launched on a career of designing for expectant mothers.

The first time I heard an eager young wife say, "Oh, you don't know what it means to me to have my husband's business friends to dinner and not feel a freak!" I knew I had found more than a living. I realized how right my grandfather was. I was filling a real need: here was a definite service.

Maternity and its problems became my chief concern, and for this women flocked to me and wrote when they moved away.

The business was almost more than I could handle when I met the man who was to shape the rest of my life. Albert Malsin was born on the Baltic shores, had studied engineering in Germany and had travelled widely. We were married in 1909. He had vision; he saw the true future of the business.

"Already," he insisted, "some of the ladies haven't got their figures back and want you to hide that fact too! We can make clothes for larger figures just as you do for expectant mothers, because all these unhappy women must dress."

Yes—all these *unhappy* women! Heavy women who couldn't

or wouldn't diet were asking me: "Surely, you can do something. . . . Make me an armhole that doesn't cut like a saw!" Such tasks inspired me. Since I had hated the business end, it was best to let Albert take over.

Besides, in four years, we had three children, and for their sake we moved to the suburbs. But I continued to design new models at the store until a few weeks before each child was born—sporting my own best expectancy clothes.

It was Albert who started our famous mail-order business from my correspondence. He put in ready-to-wear clothes, contracting with garment workers to make them to his specifications. This new venture I supervised carefully, fearful that the personal finish would be lost. And each time he told at dinner table of a new high in sales, he would lean back and roar with laughter; "And for this, I studied engineering!"

But it didn't seem so funny to me. Yet the business had grown so beyond anything I had anticipated, that I left financial matters almost entirely to my husband. The children needed me as they were growing and I devoted myself chiefly to them, though I continued to follow the progress of the business each day.

One wedding anniversary Albert gave me a painting which he had bought in Europe on one of his trips. It is a very beautiful thing—a study of a Patriarch reading from the Talmud by candlelight From my first sight of it, I was looking upon my grandfather. He might have posed for it. And who knows but the artist may have met him in his travels? It seemed to me a definite message. Those calm Old Testament eyes looked at me with quiet blessing. Again, as of old, I could hear his voice filling the room with prayer. It brought me reassurance.

We enjoyed our home life, for Albert was basically a family man. We brought up our children in the faith of our fathers. Passover was a great yearly occasion. I sat at one end of the table, all in white; it was a gala feast with as many as thirty or forty friends celebrating with us. And that picture of "my grandfather" seemed to preside.

In 1923, Albert died, after a two weeks illness. But he had built a secure foundation for us all.

Today at sixty-seven, my family has grown and there are ten grandchildren. The five thousand fellow workers at Lane Bryant share our success and our pride in filling a true need. I have been working since I was fifteen and it has been a good and rewarding life. I like best to know the service will go on, for there is always work to be done.

THE LORD'S WORK, HENRY FORD AND I

by

Perry Hayden

A simple, spiritual formula revitalized the business of Perry Hayden. And that isn't all. It made him a dynamic and forceful, as well as a radiantly happy individual. Mr. Hayden is president of the Hayden Flour Mills, Tecumseh, Michigan. Henry Ford helped him too as this interesting story relates.

I RECOMMEND TAKING GOD IN PARTNERSHIP. HE HAS BLESSED MY business, my family and me, spiritually, physically and financially. Very few are the mornings when I do not take time to get up before the rest of the household and to ask God to lead the way during the day. I keep a little card called my *"Guidance,"* upon which I write down the "directions" for the day, as they come to me in this devotional period.

God was real to me as a lad, and He is more real than ever today.

In 1930, when I was twenty-nine years old, I attended a Christian Endeavor Conference in Columbus, Ohio. The speaker on Saturday afternoon spoke directly to me. It was a challenge to surrender all I had to the Lord and let Him work in and through me. I wanted to be a successful flour miller. I wanted to make money. But how could I make money and go to China as a missionary at the same time? It was something I couldn't understand until I waited till after the meeting and asked the speaker what he would advise me to do. He knew my situation, and gave me some mighty good advice.

He said, "Perry, you go home and make all the money you can make, honestly. Then you give all the money you can give, and MIND THE LORD." I have followed that advice for the past fifteen years, and they have been the happiest years possible. Two years later, someone mailed me a little booklet on *"Tithing."* I had not heard of it before, but it sounded reasonable and I began to practice it. It brought happiness and wealth, just as God promised it would.

Then, in 1935, came the opportunity to take over control of the family business, which was then called the Wm. Hayden Milling Co. I wanted to prove to the world that a man could be a Christian and a successful business man at the same time. But I had been running this 100-year-old business but a few months when I came to the greatest crisis in my life. I was losing money, and losing it fast. Believe me, it was a humbling experience to realize how incapable I was of stopping the trend that was leading to bankruptcy. But I faithfully tithed ten per cent of my weekly pay check and kept asking God to show me the way out.

In 1936 the firm was placed under the control of a group of creditors. They were a grand bunch of men. I guess they thought it was a little strange when I suggested that we open our monthly meetings with a word of prayer. But none of them doubted my sincerity, even if they did question my ability. To make a long story short, we were out of the woods in 1937, and I was "boss" again. God did just as He said He would in the 3rd Chapter of *Malachi*, and my faith was stronger than ever.

After the business got into the "black" again, and we were making just fair progress, I heard an interesting sermon. It was on Sunday morning, September 22, 1940, in the Tecumseh Friends Church. A student preacher brought the message that morning and his text was *John* 12:24—"Verily, verily I say unto you, except a corn of wheat fall into the ground and die, it abideth alone, but IF IT DIE IT BRINGETH FORTH MUCH FRUIT."

It was wheat planting time in Michigan. Being a miller, and being interested in actually proving God in a rather unique way, I was led to do something the following Thursday that has since been heard of all the way around the world I had a few kernels of wheat actually planted, a cubic inch measure. There were just 360 kernels in the little measure. And it takes 2,150 cubic inches to make a bushel, so you can see how small a beginning this wheat project actually had.

When we planted the wheat September 26, 1940, on a plot four feet by eight feet, I told those who were present that in 1941 we were going to "tithe" the crop, and replant it. I was taking *Malachi* 3 10 seriously. Furthermore, it did appear reasonable that we could carry this project on for six years, because it said in *Leviticus* 25 3 and 4, to "sow the field" for six years and let it rest the seventh. So, armed with these biblical injunctions regarding "rebirth," "tithing," and the "sabbath," our little Dynamic Kernels Tithing wheat project got under way.

In 1941 we cut the "world's smallest wheatfield" with a sickle, cut the heads off with a pair of shears, and threshed it with a carpet-beater, and blew out the chaff with lung power. The result was a crop of fifty cubic inches! We were pleased and, of course, immediately turned over the tenth to the local Quaker Church, and replanted the remaining forty-five cubic inches in September of 1941.

In the summer of 1942 we cut the second crop with old-fashioned cradles, and found the yield was fifty-five fold, or seventy pounds. Again, we "tithed" the wheat and replanted the remaining 63 pounds on land that, for the third year in succession, had been furnished by Henry Ford, who owned a large farm near Tecumseh.

In 1943, this acre of land yielded 16 bushels from the one bushel of seed. Henry Ford himself came out to see the wheat cut, and furnished a reaper to cut it and an old-fashioned horse-power thresher from his famous Edison Institute Museum at Greenfield

Village, to thresh it. Not only that, but Henry Ford again furnished land for the fourth crop.

In 1944, this crop on fourteen acres yielded 380 bushels. Again, the tenth of the crop was "tithed" and the remaining cleaned and replanted. Henry Ford furnished the land for the fifth crop. It was 230 acres.

In the summer of 1945 a fleet of forty combines one day were sent out to the wheat field by Ford and threshed the crop of Dynamic Kernels. The yield was 5,555 bushels. The value of this little fifth crop at the market price of wheat of $1.55 per bushel, when harvested, was $8,610.25. The tithe of $861.03 went to the Friends Church who, in turn, gave it to the Tecumseh Hospital.

And now comes the thrilling outcome of this demonstration. After Henry Ford turned over the fifth crop of 5,555 bushels and it was tithed, the 5,000 bushels of seed remaining were sold to 276 farmers, representing thirty religious faiths and creeds, who planted this seed on 2,666 acres, agreeing at the time to tithe the 1946 crop to their own church.

By proclamation of Governor Kelly of Michigan, August 1, 1946 was declared Biblical Wheat Day. On that day we celebrated the sixth and final harvest of 72,150 bushels of wheat, worth at that time approximately $150,000. A large portion of the tithe, together with added gifts of other interested persons, was sent to Europe for famine relief.

I feel that one of the most significant statements ever made about tithing was uttered by Mr. Ford to a friend of his, as this project was drawing to its close. He said, "I believe the lesson we taught on tithing at Tecumseh, Michigan, will eclipse any other of my accomplishments."

How thrilled I was on different occasions when visiting with Mr. Ford to have him say—"You had faith, didn't you?" or "You are being led, aren't you?" Many times he said, "This thing is going around the world." How well I remember the last words he spoke to me as he stepped in his car and drove away from the wheat field, "God is within you."

BETTER PEOPLE
AND BETTER COWS

by

Howard W. Selby

"And better people make better farms, because somehow God and a prosperous farm just seem to go together," Howard Selby relates. Mr. Selby, a life-long leader in the farm co-operative movement, is president of the Walker-Gordon Laboratories of New England, Inc., and since 1934 General Manager of the United Farmers Co-operative Creamery Association, Inc., in Boston, Massachusetts.

A MAN MAY ENGAGE IN BUSINESS FOR ONE OF THREE REASONS. One is to make money—never mind how, so long as he does not tangle with the law. Another is to make money decently and scrupulously within popular respect. A third is to produce something better in the world—and at the same time make money.

I hold to the latter purpose; that the object of business is not only to make a fair and honest living but to help make people better and happier. Many a man who once thought that business and religion did not mix has discovered otherwise. Many a man has found that the practice of religion pays. But one cannot take it up with the sole motive of becoming more successful. He cannot adopt religion as he would a new accounting system.

I wish all business men realized that it is not only good religion but also the best kind of business to serve humanity and make God their partner. I believe that God may require one man to engage in business for the same object that He calls another to serve in the pulpit.

I happen to be in the milk producing business. Our co-operative dairy association seeks to raise milk production among its members to the highest possible standard and volume—which means raising the standard of our producing herds. We want better cows, but I doubt that we'll have better cows without better men. If this sounds like an eccentric statement, let me risk another· there is a direct relationship between religion and the dairy business. In place after place I have seen the standard and quality of milk advance after the standards and quality of a community have improved Religion makes better men; and better men in a dairying community are interested in developing better cows. It is all of a pattern, with God as a center. An earnest Christian is never content with the average or with mediocrity; he strives always to excel.

In a Vermont meadow, one of our co-operative's farmers pointed out to me a weather-beaten dilapidated farmhouse several fields away. "A generation ago," he said, "that was a prosperous farm. Fine, upstanding people lived there. The place had no mortgage upon it, and its family had money in the bank. Anyone in the neighborhood in need of a thousand dollars could borrow from those people at any time. Now it is a marginal farm under the burden of a heavy mortgage. Its owner is poor, struggling, and constantly in debt."

"Yes," I broke in, "I think I can complete the picture, although I don't know the people. The family which lived there a generation ago got up early on Sunday morning to do the chores. Then the team was harnessed to the buckboard and driven to the crossroads church. But the family now living there is bound down by the burden of the place. Those people never seem to get their chores done because of their mental attitude, so they don't get time to go to church. Much of their trouble is worry. They left God out of their lives, and the mental burden crushed the spirit out of them. The older family had God for a partner—and the driving power which led it to success."

"That's right!" said my farmer friend. "You've described the situation exactly. Somehow, God and a prosperous farm seem to go together."

We hope soon to install a personnel man whose job will be what the preachers might call evangelistic. He will work with the practical side of our manpower situation, but his chief purpose will be something higher. He will have social ideals, and will seek to bring labor and management to an understanding of each other. He will try to show the laborer that he must give a full, honest day's work for his pay, and he will show management that they must be fair in all their dealings with labor. But perhaps his greatest function will be to put romance into this business and emphasize the dignity and importance of each worker's individual task.

For example, here is a man whose job is to bottle milk day after day. Perhaps his job has become quite humdrum—just bottling milk and covering it with a cap. He needs a vision of where that bottle goes, that it will help to nourish the life of a beautiful baby, that it will be a factor in creating the wonderful, clean, healthy youth of America, that it will help to grow a great citizenship and to develop the greatest country in the world. Thus a bottle of milk is an important factor in the development of American civilization.

Our co-operative, which includes several hundred farmers, holds regular group and sectional meetings for discussion of common problems and better operating methods. I always prepare for these meetings by having a period of prayer and meditation. I ask God to guide us in the meetings and am sure He does so.

In weekly radio talks to our farmers, I always quote passages from scripture as reminders of the place that God occupies in the cycle of better cows, better and more milk, better barns, better roads, better schools, better communities, and better men raising better cows. There is always the background recognition that God is the answer to all these problems. Good pastures, good herds, good people—that is our working formula; and it is inspiring how it helps to develop men and raise the vision and self-respect of our member families. That formula has encouraged many a member to advance himself from depressed circumstances into community responsibility and leadership.

Community responsibility and self-respect inspire pride in good appearance, without which there can't be much sanitation around a dairy farm. When a farmer gets his sheds cleaned up and whitewashed, invariably his house stands out like a sore thumb if it too has not been properly cared for. His newly-aroused sense of pride is touched, with the result that he won't be satisfied until his house looks as neat as his farm buildings.

When sheds and barns and houses are painted and in good repair, almost automatically the people around them begin to show improvement. It must be true that "cleanliness is next to Godliness." I believe also that cleanliness leads to Godliness. For decay in anything no matter what it is—leads to corruption.

Repaint, repair, rebuild, clean up, transform, arrest decay in a barn, in a house—in a man, in a community—all are part of a cycle of renewed growth. This creative pattern belongs to God's work with humanity—and to men of business who do God's work.

Sorrows Needn't Get You Down

MESSAGE TO THE BEREAVED

by

Natalie Kalmus

"Death never again can frighten me," Natalie Kalmus states as she gives readers her glimpse into the wonderful truth about everlasting life. Mrs. Kalmus is color director for Technicolor Motion Corporation which she helped found and organize. She is in complete charge of color for all motion pictures made here and abroad by Technicolor.

"DON'T WORRY, BUT COME TO ME AS SOON AS YOU CAN," MY SIS-
ter, Eleanor Smith, wired. At the time I was in London working
out Technicolor problems with one of the British motion picture
companies.

I felt a deep, numbing pang. I knew Eleanor had been ill some
time. Surely this was her gentle way of telling me the end was
coming.

I could not picture—or accept it. Always radiating charm,
friendliness and an inner happiness, my sister had been a wonderful inspiration to those close to her. She had that rare trait of
always giving others a pat on the back, lifting their spirits and
sending them off with a fresh outlook on life.

When first stricken by the most fearsome of medical enemies,
the doctors had told her that her days were numbered. Knowing
this had not made the slightest difference in her warm interest in
people—nor in her deep abiding faith in the wonder of God.

But now she needed me. I returned to the States and hurried to Eleanor, expecting to find her in bed in great pain. Instead she was in the living room perched jauntily on the sofa, looking more like a school girl of seventeen than an incurably ill woman.

"Natalie," she held out her arms joyously, "I'm so happy now that you're here. We have so much to talk over." To anyone listening I might have dropped in for a casual call.

After Eleanor had later retired for the night, the doctor drew me aside. "Mrs. Kalmus," he said, "I think that it will be a most trying experience for you if you stay here through to the end. I'm afraid that your sister's last hours will be an agony of pain."

Medically I knew he was right. Yet the exquisite radiance I noticed in my sister's face seemed somehow to refute his statement. The strange feeling swept over me that the strength of my sister's spirit could well triumph over her pain.

During the next few days I discovered that Eleanor was doing many things to baffle the doctors. They were preparing her for some very grim final moments. She was ignoring their solemn suggestions and remedies. One night she had me sit down on the side of her bed.

"Natalie, promise me that you won't let them give me any drugs. I realize that they are trying to help relieve my pain, but I want to be fully aware of every sensation. *I am convinced that death will be a beautiful experience.*"

I promised. Alone later, I wept, thinking of her courage. Then as I tossed in bed on through the night, I realized that what I looked to be a calamity, my sister intended to be a triumph.

One afternoon Eleanor, in the most airy and lighthearted manner, asked several friends to a dinner party which she, on the spur of the moment, decided to hold. I was stunned. But Eleanor grinned at me impishly in high spirits. The sight of the happiness in her face checked my objections.

On the night of the party Eleanor dressed meticulously, concealing the pain I knew she felt. We helped her downstairs before the guests were to arrive. Sitting in a turquoise chair in her yellow evening gown, she sparkled with life and gaiety. Again I noticed the school girl look on her face.

The party was a grand success; the guests were never once aware of the illness which my sister concealed so expertly. That night, however, when she was carried to bed, her deep physical weariness appeared on the surface. Then I realized that my sister knew this was her final social fling. She had planned it that way.

Ten days later the final hour drew near. I had been at her bedside for hours. We had talked about many things, and always I marveled at her quiet, sincere confidence in eternal life. Not once did the physical torture inside overcome her spiritual strength. This was something that the doctors simply hadn't taken into account.

"Dear kind God, keep my mind clear and give me peace," she had murmured over and over again during those last days.

We had talked so long that I noticed she was drifting off to sleep. I left her quietly with the nurse and retired to get some rest. A few minutes later I heard my sister's voice calling for me. Quickly I returned to her room. She was dying.

I sat on her bed and took her hand. It was on fire. Then she seemed to rise up in bed almost to a sitting position.

"Natalie," she said, "there are so many of them. There's Fred . . . and Ruth—what's she doing here? Oh, I know!"

An electric shock went through me. She had said Ruth! Ruth was her cousin who had died suddenly the week before. *But Eleanor had not been told of Ruth's sudden death.*

Chill after chill shot up and down my spine. I felt on the verge of some powerful, almost frightening knowledge. She *had* murmured Ruth's name.

Her voice was surprisingly clear. "It's so confusing. So many of them!" Suddenly her arms stretched out as happily as when she had welcomed me! "I'm going up," she murmured.

Then she dropped her arms around my neck—and relaxed in

my arms. *The will of her spirit had turned final agony into rapture.*

As I lay her head back on the pillow, there was a warm, peaceful smile on her face. Her golden brown hair lay carelessly on the pillow. I took a white flower from the vase and placed it in her hair. With her petite, trim figure, her wavy hair, the white flower, and the soft smile, she looked once more—and permanently—just like a school girl.

Never again will death frighten me in any way. This was my sister's inheritance to me—her final, beautiful gift. I had seen for myself how thin was the curtain between life and death. I had glimpsed part of the wonderful truth about everlasting life.

In the weeks that followed, however, there was a tremendous vacuum inside me which I could not fill. Then, as though heaven-sent, a famous authoress came to visit me and brought me a prayer by Rudolph Steinert, written to comfort those grief-stricken by the death of loved-ones.

I read the words slowly, letting them settle deep inside me. Soon many facts became clear. Without realizing it, I had been desperately trying to hold on to my sister, which was fair to neither of us. It might well be handicapping Eleanor in her efforts to adjust to her new life. It was upsetting my own normal life. With this realization a new peace and tranquillity began to fill the emotional vacuum inside me.

A perfect relationship now exists between my sister and me. Frequently, I feel her comforting presence. At the same time I am again able to draw full satisfaction and enjoyment from both my business and social life. Whenever the opportunity arises, I am happy to share the remarkable story of my sister's passing with others for the help and comfort it can give them. And always I have the feeling that it is Eleanor herself who is passing on this beautiful understanding of death—*through me.*

As for those occasions when loneliness assails me, I say the words of this prayer over and over to myself as I remember them:

Into thy new surroundings let my love be woven.
Warming thy coolness, cooling thy warmness,
Live upward bourne by love, illuminated by light.

The beautiful love we found
I shall now send into the realms of the spirit
To link soul with soul when, from the spirits' illuminous lands,
Thou wilt turn in search of what thou seekest in me
Thou wilt find my love in thinking.

I TELL YOU
THEY HAVE NOT DIED

by

Geoffrey O'Hara

A train roaring through the night . . . the steady rhythm of rolling wheels . . and the music to a great song is born. Geoffrey O'Hara, one of America's famous composers, tells the thrilling story behind his creation of the inspiring spiritual song "There Is No Death." And what American has not sung Mr. O'Hara's familiar "K-K-K-Katy"?

YEARS AGO A CONCERT SINGER CAME TO ME WITH A DEEPLY MOVing story. A skeptic would have casually passed off the tale he told, but I listened intently. Music is a strong bond between people. Moreover, his story was about my song, "There Is No Death."

The tale he told concerned his mother. She had married an irresponsible man who immediately left her. After this marriage her father had disowned her, but when he discovered that she was destitute, he let her return—to live in a chicken coop which he had made over with a bed and scattered articles of furniture. In this chicken coop the singer-to-be was born. His mother died in childbirth.

When the young boy grew up, he decided to take up singing as a career. Soon he acquired a fine reputation, toured the country, and always at the close of the program he would sing, "There Is No Death."

At this point the man's voice quickened with excitement as he gripped my arm tensely. "Mr. O'Hara, just before I sing this song the most amazing thing always happens. My mother appears by my side. I can see her as well as I see you now She smiles at me and places her soft hand on my shoulder. I feel it as surely as you feel my hand on your arm. She stands by my side until I finish the song. Then she is gone. . . ."

It would take a cold-blooded man not to respond to his story. I didn't mention that the words in the song affected me with the same electric effect, that shock waves coursed up and down my body when I wrote the music to these powerful words. This man's experience was similar to many others I have heard, all from people who had either lost their fear of death after listening to the song, or from those who had felt a similar contact with a departed loved one.

The story behind the composition of "There Is No Death" is equally powerful and moving. The words were written by my friend, the late Gordon Johnstone, who penned the lyrics to many of my songs. Four people, including an Army colonel, Gordon Johnstone, myself, and the publisher, Walter Eastman, played a prominent part in the story.

In 1919 Gordon Johnstone met a retired Canadian Army colonel whose command had been wiped out in a series of bloody battles. At first, feeling the loss of his men to the marrow of his bones, the colonel was bitterly despondent. Then slowly his attitude of abject despair had changed to one of quiet faith—a faith in God and in eternal life, because, the colonel said, "I began to feel their breath, their hands touched mine as I walked down the trenches. I could hear their voices. I tell you they have not died . . ."

Something about this hardboiled colonel's faith—his confidence in the "other world" where his men now laughed and talked together—inspired Johnstone. The words "I tell you they have not died" raced through Johnstone's brain as he rode back to his home that same night. He discovered verses forming on his lips. No sooner had he reached his house than he rushed to the telephone and called his publisher. Then without having written a line down on paper, he poured forth the words to "There Is No Death" over the telephone to Walter Eastman.

"I tell you they have not died,
They live and breathe with you;
They walk here at your side,
They tell you things are true.
Why dream of poppied sod
When you can feel their breath,
When Flow'r and soul and God
Know there is no death.

"I tell you they have not died,
Their hands clasp yours and mine;
They are but glorified,
They have become divine.
They live! they know! they see!
They shout with every breath:
All is eternal life!
There is no death!" *

Walter Eastman, head of the New York Agency of Chappell & Company, London publishers, listened to the words and was also gripped by their great intensity. Having lost his brother in the war, they struck him with the impact of a howitzer. I was then called in, and the three of us agreed that it was a song to be fashioned with "reinforced concrete." The great positive truth in the words had to burst on the listener with a smashing effect. "I tell you they have not died . . ."

The challenge was powerful, too important to call for any quick tune that I might hammer out. I realized that I must await a proper "inspiration." Day after day I took out the words, read them over, groped, strained . . . Several times I did compose complete music, but in each case, three times in all, I tore up the results. When the right music came to me, I would know it beyond

* Copyright Chappell & Co. 1919.

any possible doubt. (Editor's note—During this period Mr. O'Hara did manage to compose thirty-two other numbers all of which have since been published.)

How many composers have so grappled and struggled with a song! Then quite unexpectedly the solution fairly clouts them between the eyes. And where does it often happen? On a train. Riding over wheels seems to create a steady rhythm that soon dissolves into a sublime silence.

While travelling thus from Boston to New York four months after receiving the words to "There Is No Death," I slipped into such a relaxed state. On a hunch I brought out the words again and read them over. Suddenly, like the shock of a plunge into an icy lake, the music came to me, numbing me all over. Feverishly I wrote. By the time I reached New York I had the framework of the song finished.

That same evening I retired at 9 P.M. in order to be fresh in the morning when I planned to finish the piano accompaniment and do the final inking job. The hours ticked away—ten, eleven, twelve, one o'clock—but I could not sleep. The summons was too strong to deny. I arose and went to work.

As I toiled on through the night, I felt that a battery was attached to my chair and was sending a steady current coursing through my body. Never have I experienced such a strong spiritual force driving me on. Never before or after did I do my composing at such an unusual hour.

At three o'clock in the morning I finished the song, and not a note was changed from that moment on. The next morning I took the music without delay to Walter Eastman, the publisher, and played it for him. His reaction was unusual as had been all the experiences connected with "There Is No Death." He listened to it quietly, then without a word picked up the song, put it in the safe, turned the lock, and walked out of the building. Such eloquent silence meant more to me than any words.

God was good to me when He gave me talent to compose music. Perhaps I can pay off some of my debt to Him through my songs.

I believe that a song should say something, and if the message has a useful effect on people, then may I not feel that I have made a contribution to the world? In many cases I have discovered that it is not the serious songs that do the most good. Sometimes a quiet humor or expression of a simple sentiment in a song can be of great stimulus. "K-K-K-Katy" which I composed in 1917 proved popular with the soldiers, and I like to think it did much for their morale.

"There Is No Death" and "K-K-K-Katy" are contrasts in songs, but each made its contribution. So, too, may contrasting views of religion offer a contribution to all mankind, for by understanding different viewpoints we can come to a really great understanding of God.

SAY IT WITH FLOWERS

by

Henry Penn

From street urchin to owner of one of the most successful floral establishments in the country— that's the story of Henry Penn. The famous slogan "Say it with flowers" was the direct outgrowth of an idea conceived by Mr Penn, who is the past president of the Society of American Florists and current president of the Beacon Street Temple in Boston, Massachusetts.

WHEN I WAS TEN YEARS OLD I WORKED AFTER SCHOOL HOURS IN Boston as a newsboy. One evening a man pushed a hand cart up to the curb It was loaded with white pond lilies. I had never seen anything so beautiful!

The man then asked us to sell the lilies on the street at five cents a bunch. We were to collect a cent and a half for each bunch we sold. Just holding them in my hands made me tingle all over. The only flowers I had ever seen before were in public gardens behind "Don't Touch" signs.

At that moment I decided I wanted to be a florist. Two years later I had a cart, and the newsboys were working for me, selling flowers I bought from florists at the end of the day.

As I worked hard to develop my own business, I also began to acquire a better understanding of people. For through flowers one can learn many things about human beings.

Flowers have been the language of faith, hope, sympathy and happiness since the beginning of time. People in their highest spiritual moments have turned to flowers to express their deepest emotions.

Being a florist I know this to be true. I also knew that flowers can transform the lives of people. Next to my office desk is a chair which I call my "Confessional Chair." Here people have seated themselves and revealed to me amazing stories of their lives. Confessions, fears, hopes—I have listened to them all. People seem to open up their hearts when they are sending flowers—even when they are near flowers.

One incident I'll never forget happened many years ago. I have told this story many times, but it is just as poignant today as when it happened back in the depression period.

One afternoon three children entered my shop, two boys and a girl. They were about ten years old, raggedly dressed, but at this moment well scrubbed. One of the boys took off his cap, gazed about the store somewhat doubtfully, then came up to me.

"Sir, we'd like something in yellow flowers."

Something in their tense, nervous manner made me think that this was a very special occasion. I showed them some inexpensive yellow spring flowers.

The boy who had assumed the spokesman role for the group shook his head with decision. "I think we'd like something better than that."

"Do they have to be yellow?" I asked.

"Yes, sir," he said. "You see, Mister, Mickey would like 'em better if they were yellow. He had a yellow sweater. I guess he liked yellow better'n any other color."

"Are they for his funeral?" I asked quietly.

The boy nodded, suddenly choked up. The little girl was desperately struggling to keep back the tears.

"She's his sister," the boy said. "He was a swell little kid. A truck hit him yesterday while he was playin' in the street." His lips were now trembling.

The other boy now entered the conversation. "Us kids in his block took up a collection. We got eighteen cents," he added proudly. "Would roses cost an awful lot, sir—yellow roses, I mean?"

I smiled suddenly. "It just happens that I have some nice yellow roses here that I'm offering special today for eighteen cents a dozen." I pointed into the flower case.

"Gee, those would be swell!"

"Yes, Mickey'd sure like those." The spirits of the committee suddenly rose as they gazed at the stately, golden roses in the case.

"I'll make up a nice spray with ferns and ribbons. Where do you want me to send them?" I asked.

"Would it be all right, Mister, if we took 'em with us?" one of the boys asked. "We'd kinda like to—you—know—give 'em to Mickey ourselves. He'd like it better that way."

I fixed up the spray, accepted the eighteen cents gravely, and watched the youngsters trudge out of the store. My spirits were uplifted for days afterwards. I realized then, as I have often sensed it, the warm exultation of God's presence.

What is it that fills people with such a haunting yearning for flowers at certain times? Very frequently I get scrawls on note paper, scribbles on pieces of cardboard or used envelopes, sent from hospitals and other public institutions.

"Have you got any old flowers that you don't need?" they write. "Anything at all will do."

These people think of flowers in terms of pleasant childhood memories, past happiness, the beauty and sacredness of a decorated church, and other spiritual memories that have transcended the souls of men and women.

Several years ago I received regular orders from a prison convict in Jackson, Michigan. On each occasion he had us send a box of flowers to his mother in Boston. Somehow I knew that such a man was a potentially good citizen. Sure enough when he had served his time, he returned to his home and has been a useful citizen ever since.

Flowers breed love and good will. They are never associated

with hate and evil spirits. I would vote for flowers to melt down the hearts of the most hardened individuals.

For example, take the buds of two simple flowers. The florist exposes both buds to an equal amount of sunlight, water, and attention. Then for some mysterious reason one of the buds will gradually open its petals and burst into beautiful bloom, giving forth fragrant odors, while the other bud remains tight and hard, exposing no beauty and giving off no fragrance.

The opportunity to compare this strange fact of nature to human beings occurred one night during a banquet given to raise a large sum of money for a worthy cause. I was the chairman of this drive. Near me I noticed a man famous for his tightness with the purse strings. He knew he would be asked to give and was stiffening his resistance. Then with startling clarity I saw a chance to use the illustration of the two buds.

There on the table was a bowl of flowers, including several beautiful roses in bloom and one or two buds which were closed tight. I took out one of each and stood up before the audience to give my speech. Then I told the story of the two buds and made the analogy to certain people who missed so much out of life because they refused to "open up"

As I developed my theme, I saw a slow smile spread over the face of the close-fisted rich man. Before the evening was over he had pledged far more than I am sure he had intended to.

I feel unhappy if the effect of flowers is overdone. I remember once when a very rich woman came to my shop and ordered ten thousand dollars worth of flowers for her daughter's coming out party. This order was almost more than I could handle.

But the very next week I had a much more satisfying and stimulating experience. A poor woman entered my shop and said she had one dollar to spend.

"I want to get the most beautiful bouquet you have in your shop to send for my daughter's graduation—for one dollar."

I put together this order myself with considerably more pleasure and zest than I felt in filling the rich lady's order. Several weeks later I received a note that is one of my treasures.

It said simply: "The bouquet of flowers you sent to my daughter was the most beautiful I have ever seen, and my friends said it must have cost ten dollars. I don't see how you can afford to send so many flowers for a dollar."

Yes, I will never understand why everybody in the world doesn't become a florist. There is no finer way to see beauty in flowers, in people, in God.

Revitalizing Your Life Through Faith

HOW MY FAITH
HAS HELPED ME

by

J. C. Penney

*J. C. Penney, whose stores dot the country, is a
business man who believes that Christianity is the
important part of every day's activity. He believes
that faith works in human affairs and has demon-
strated this belief countless times.*

ONE OF OUR STORE MANAGERS WROTE ME RECENTLY THAT THESE
times tend to fill everyone with pessimism. That should not be.
We should recognize our times for what they are: periods of
tribulation but not of pessimism. They should inspire us to re-
examine our faiths and to re-establish our convictions more firmly.
As long as we have any faith at all in God, we must know that He
is all-powerful, that justice and right are His will for the world
and that eventually His purpose will be established here on earth.
Good emerges slowly, but we must not doubt its final outcome.

And just as with individuals, so as a nation will our fate be determined by our choice of the hard right, instead of the easy
wrong. America was founded in prayer, in faith and in the heroic
spirit of sacrifice. Comfortable living in easy-going years tends to
soften us, and both our spiritual and our physical muscles become
flabby. Times like the present are testing periods. The harder
they become, the more determined we should be not to be infected
by doubts and fears which bedevil the world.

The present state of the world, and of people in it, does not shake my faith in the ultimate triumph of freedom and justice, for I was reared by parents whose faith in God and whose belief that right will triumph are too deeply ingrained in me to cause me to doubt. From a worldly standpoint, my parents were humble folk. My father was an old-school Baptist minister who preached the better part of his lifetime and never took one penny of remuneration for it. He earned his living as a farmer. Though brought up very strictly, I have always been thankful that my parents were God-fearing, for I learned early to honor and obey them—and to work

If I could get a message over to the youth of this country, it would be that success in life does not depend on genius. Any young man of ordinary intelligence, who is morally sound, aboveboard in his dealings, and not afraid of work, should succeed in spite of obstacles and handicaps, if he plays the game fairly and squarely and keeps everlastingly at it. The possibilities before one are measured by the determination which is within one.

For many years I selected personally our store managers. After I had satisfied myself about a prospect's character and qualifications, I inquired about his home life. Was it happy and harmonious? Did his wife have his interests at heart? Would she stand at his side and help him to attain his ambitions? If I did not believe that his wife measured up, I did not employ the man. If I found that his wife was a true helpmate, I felt that he would succeed, other things being equal, for a good woman's power to encourage is well-nigh unlimited.

In 1910, the mother of my two oldest sons died after a brief illness. The shock was so sudden and severe that it nearly overwhelmed me. Although I never drank liquor even moderately, I had an intense desire to drink. The reason was doubtless the unconscious desire of drowning sorrow, yet also instinctively I knew that I must not yield; that if ever the desire got one foot within the door it would come in bodily and I would go down.

The craving lasted not only for months but for years. Many a night I walked the streets, battling with grief and temptation that had fastened upon me.

This was the most critical time of my life, but the memory of my father's faith buoyed me up. His words when I first went to work—"Jim will make it; I like the way he has started out"—again and again came to my rescue.

This experience altered my viewpoint about things that matter and those which are nonessential. It enlarged my vision and increased my interest in my fellow-men. Life took on a different aspect. I had always been interested in seeing that men in our stores had their opportunities, but until then it was largely because I too benefited by their successes.

But after that experience my interest was no longer one of dollars and cents. Instead, it was an interest in the welfare and advancement of our men so that they might take their rightful places in society. I realized that money—necessary as it is—should be a means to a worthy aim and not the end in itself. Up to this time I had been in poor health but along with my change of thought—the result of a spiritual awakening—I began to develop a stronger body.

At one time during my business career I broke down, both nervously and physically, and went to a sanitarium. One night while there I had an overwhelming conviction that this was my last night of life. So sure was I that my time had come that I got up and wrote farewell letters to my family.

The next morning, however, I passed a parlor in the sanitarium and heard singing. A few people were gathered in a religious meeting. I felt the urge to enter. In great weariness of spirit I listened to the hymns, to the Scripture reading and to the prayers. Then, a profound sense of inner release came over me A heavy weight seemed lifted from my spirit. I was amazed at my change and in the days that followed I regained mental and bodily health. Perhaps the feeling of death that night was a symptom of a new man being born in me.

I do not mean to give the impression that because of these experiences I have successfully applied Christian principles to all phases of my life. It is true that God has blessed me beyond what I deserve. Because our company has been conscientious in practice of the Golden Rule, success has blessed our business. I feel ashamed, however, that in other ways I have not followed Christ's teachings as well as I might. I have not loved God as I should. I neglected my obligations to the Church until recent years. I certainly have not worked for the brotherhood of man outside my business to the degree that should be expected of a good Christian. But I am now trying earnestly to make up for what I failed to do.

The practice of Christian principles was desirable when our company was started. But even some men who did not practice them succeeded. In my early days, one could put religion in one compartment of his life, his business relations in another, and gain a measure of success. But it is not true in the same way today. I believe that the stepped-up business cycle, a product of the industrial revolution and mass production, make this practice today a virtual necessity.

Those who have the greater part of their adult life before them should study with great earnestness the relation between Christ's two commandments—to love God and to love your neighbor as yourself With such a balance of these two great laws worked out in one's everyday life, you may be sure of a life of spiritual blessing and, I hope, one of material prosperity.

PEACE THROUGH FAITH

by

William Green

*William Green, one of America's most honored
labor leaders, testifies how religion has helped him
in his half century of labor leadership. Mr. Green
is president of the American Federation of Labor.*

DURING MORE THAN HALF A CENTURY OF ENDEAVOR TO IMPROVE
the condition of working people in this country, I have found
my personal religion a source of strength and comfort. Religion
brings peace in the midst of turmoil.

By *personal* religion I do not mean a private religion, an experience separate from association with my fellow men. I strongly
doubt that there is any such thing as a private religion, any more
than there can be a private language. By its very essence, religion
is social and has primary and direct bearing upon one's associ-
ations with others.

A religion distinct from ethics and morals becomes empty
ritualism and sinks quickly to the level of primitive magic. This
oneness of experience with God and experience with men is what
the Prophet Micah meant when he proclaimed: "He hath showed
thee, O Man, what is good; and what doth Jehovah require of
thee but to do justly, and to love kindness, and to walk humbly
with thy God?"

I suppose that a casual observer examining my record might
conclude that my life has been one of turmoil and strife. I cannot
deny that it has been one of struggle.

When I reached seventeen, I followed the trade of my father

[113]

and went to work in coal mines of the Southern Ohio fields. I also joined immediately the struggle to better the lot of the men and the families they supported by toiling in the dark and damp of subterranean pits. Neither the work nor attempts to improve working conditions were exactly peaceful. The mines were dangerous; so were the picket lines.

My father and mother brought with them from across the sea an intense loyalty to the people with whom they lived and worked. They brought also a deep sense of their duty to God. A combination of this loyalty and this duty made a priceless heritage left me by God-fearing parents. Every morning and evening at six, Father led us in family devotions. Mother's life revolved around the union, the Baptist Church and the family.

In those days a strike might last from three to ten months. Miners' families helped each other out, even so, we went hungry every now and then. I also saw anguish mingled with fear lay hold of a family when fellow workers carried home a broken body, following one of the horrible accidents that were so frequent in the mines. I saw what it meant to mothers and small children when the breadwinner was taken away or injured so that he could not work. In those days the law did not hold an employer responsible for what might befall his workmen. When I was sent to the State Senate a few years later, I resolved to hit that failure and hit it hard. My proposal for a workingman's compensation law was greeted with cries of "socialism" and termed an attack upon the American system. I learned what it meant to be "despised and rejected of men."

Many times in years that followed casual onlookers might conclude that there could be no peace for one so near the center of struggles that marked the efforts of American working men and women to improve their lot. In many of these I was called to play a leading part. But throughout it all, there has been a way of inner peace. This way is the way of faith in the common people and faith in God.

How can one have faith in God and not have faith in man, who is the child of God? I have seen the twisted, distorted nature of man at its worst, striving for wealth, position and power. And yet my faith is continually being restored by seeing the common people of this country in loyal and sacrificial devotion to the cause of their mutual betterment. Although I have seen grasping, self-seeking, evil-designing men in all walks of life, I have also discovered that when plain, everyday folk are given a way to make their desires felt, they invariably straighten things out. Right will prevail.

Faith in God, faith in man, I cannot say which comes first. I heard recently of a farmer who lived in that section of Michigan called the "Thumb." Spring comes late up there, because that section is almost completely surrounded by icy waters. One particularly late spring, this farmer announced to his neighbors that he was convinced that spring would not come at all that year. When they asked him why, he replied, "Everyone knows it can't get warm until the ice gets out of Lake Michigan, and how is the ice going to get out until it gets warm?"

The facts as this simple man observed them presented one of those closed "vicious circles." He failed to realize that his little thumb of land was only a small part of a great, wide world, in which, revolving in its course around the eternal sun, were set in motion cosmic forces far beyond his ken. Many times during the last fifty years the cause of right and justice seemed hedged in. Efforts to free it were blocked by a vicious circle, and there seemed no way out. Today, in many ways, the world seems to be dead-locked. Having won a victory in war, we wonder whether we can summon enough good will and intelligence to win victories which belong to peace.

In perplexing times like these, I find again and again that I must rely on faith—faith that if all of us do our utmost there will be forces far beyond our ken that are at work for good in the great universe about us. The stars in their courses fight for right. The ice will melt, and summer will come.

So it has been that in the midst of strife I have found peace. Faith in God, faith in man. Like the bow and the violin, together they make harmony.

JACK MINER'S
BIRD MISSIONARIES

by

Manly F. Miner

Ever hear of "religious geese"? Manly Miner, son of the late Jack Miner who founded the Jack Miner Bird Sanctuary at Kingsville, Ontario, tells the fascinating story of these winged messengers of God.

LIKE MANY FAMOUS PERSONALITIES, JACK MINER WAS A RELI-gious man. I think often of two of his original sayings One was: "I never started living until I started believing"; and the other· "My bird sanctuary would never have been what it is, nor have gained world recognition, had I not taken God into partnership and given Him first place." Always he would add. "I owe everything to God." When he died, he said, "I am just going on ahead."

Back in 1904 Jack Miner started feeding, protecting and caring for bird life. He established the Jack Miner Sanctuary at Kingsville, Ontario. In 1909 he began banding birds, and was the pioneer bander on this continent to obtain a complete record of when and where banded birds were shot and killed. The banding was begun and the record of returns from the bands kept for the purpose of securing authentic information regarding migration seasons, migration routes, length of life of the wildfowl, and other such hitherto unknown information. The data secured in the thirty-seven years in which his system has been followed provides now a vast fund of scientific knowledge which has been made available to institutions of learning throughout the Dominion and the United States

In the year 1914 there was incorporated in his bird banding scheme a feature which made it unique and also successful beyond his dreams Let me tell you the beginning of that in Jack Miner's own words:

"Early one morning, like a star shooting across the heavens, God's radio—or God's guidance, if you wish to call it that—said to me, 'Stamp verses of Scripture on the blank side of your duck and goose bands' From the very first time I stamped such a verse on a band I felt the help of God and knew I now had my tagging system complete"

That spring he started doing this. Nothing was heard of his "religious geese," as the neighborhood boys called them, until early in the fall. Then he received a telegram from Rev. W. G. Walton of Cochrane, Ontario, at that time the most northerly railroad station. The message read: "Am on my way to your home with several bands placed on birds by you and taken off by Indians and Eskimos in the Arctic Circle."

A couple of days later this devout missionary arrived at our home I shall never forget the scene: he and my father sitting in front of our fireplace, and he putting his hand into a pocket pulling out the bands and giving them to my father!

Mr. Walton told us that for twenty-six years he had been working on the east coast of Hudson's Bay. In that bleak land he had performed the same duties as had Sir Wilfred Grenfell in Labrador. In all those years he never had been "outside," or, as we say it, to the scenes of civilization.

As he laid the priceless bands in my father's hands, he said, "But, Mr. Miner, I had to come out now. These verses from the Holy Book have caused a great revival and awakening of religious feeling among our native Indians and Eskimos. I had to come and tell you of it. They all believe these are messages sent direct from

God—as indeed they are! They come to me to interpret the messages."

The verses imprinted on the bands were ones that were favorites of Jack Miner's, usually promises, such as. "No good thing will He withhold from them that walk uprightly", or, "Have faith in God." So many geese bearing Jack Miner's Scripture-verse bands have been shot by the Cree Indians and Eskimos of the Hudson's Bay district in the last thirty years that the Mission houses have always been filled with men and women eager to learn "what God has said this time."

Following that visit Mr. Walton gladly acted as Jack Miner's agent in collecting the bands, and hundreds of them were returned to us that never would have been kept had it not been for the verse stamped upon them.

Since Mr Walton's first visit other missionaries, namely the Jesuit priests of the Roman Catholic Church, have also co-operated wholeheartedly with us in the same manner to collect our bands. A book could be written on incidents that occurred in this connection among these people of the Far North.

In connection with the birds shot in the South, mostly throughout the Eastern half of the United States, Central America, Cuba, Haiti and the Northerly states of South America, the response to it was astonishing and very gratifying. In most cases the shooting of a fowl bearing a Scripture-stamped band is sufficiently unique as to constitute a newspaper story. Frequently it is syndicated and goes into a thousand or more newspapers, so that the message comes before the eyes of millions of persons.

One of the most remarkable letters ever to come into my father's hands was written by an inmate of the Arkansas State Prison. It read in part.

"I am in here for overdraft on a bank; my room-mate, who is sitting at my elbow, is in here for murder. We have a paper here giving an account of a duck shot in Louisiana, with your band marked, 'Have faith in God.' We have looked this up in the Bible and find the reference correct."

Many times sportsmen use these bands as watch fobs, and some whose lives have been changed make this particular use of them because, they explain, the word of God, produced casually in this unusual way, serves readily as a medium for the start of a conversation on life-changing conversion or the high things of life.

Now that my father is reaping the reward of his well-spent life, people ask, "Will the work be carried on?" In answer I am happy to say that my two brothers are as keenly interested as I am in having father's lifework perpetuated The twelve million citizens of Canada, the members of the Provincial Legislatures and the members of the Dominion Parliament as well as all Canadian Senators all are enthusiastic in their interest in this work.

Having put our bands on over 50,000 ducks and on nearly 40,000 Canada geese, the reader will readily understand that our mail is always interesting I acted as father's secretary for thirty-five years, and you can realize the magnitude of the blessing I have enjoyed in learning of men who, because of him, turned their faces toward God I have discovered that all humanity is absorbed in some phase of Christianity, even if many do not admit it. I realize very clearly what Father meant when he said, "No life is complete without God."

CONFESSION OF FAITH

by

Faith Baldwin

*"I have always known the potent power of
prayer," Faith Baldwin states "Twice I was told
that a child of mine would die . . . I prayed .
. . . my children lived" One of the most successful
and popular woman writers of our time, Faith
Baldwin's books and stories have sold in the millions and many have been made into motion pictures.*

WHEN I WAS A CHILD, MY MATERNAL GRANDMOTHER, WHO LIVED
with us, would warn me, after I had been naughty, that I would
soon get my come-uppance It never failed and I learned this the
hard way If I snitched a cookie and immediately, or hours there-
after, fell down and knocked out an infant tooth, I was experienc-
ing the law of retribution in operation.

There was no nonsense about my Grandmother—she was kind,
merciful, humorous, and very devout I have her Bible, the New
Testament, bound in several light weight, large volumes, which
her son-in-law, my father, had made for her when her hands grew
too palsied to hold a heavy book.

Often, it seems to us that the law of retribution does not work.
That is, when we grow up and see people performing like amoral,
greedy, soulless monkeys without punishment, we say, in the
usual parlance, "they get away with it." But I cannot believe that
they do, even upon earth. Which of us can look into their hearts
and see there the fear, the anxiety, and the inevitable insecurity?

My paternal grandparents were Methodist missionaries; my father, his brother, and all but one of his sisters were born in China In my grandfather's house in China and at my own home Sabbath was observed and family prayers were said each morning In my very early years my mother and father attended church regularly, and I went to Sunday School. But gradually my parents drew away from religious observance. whether it was because my father's young life had been excessively restricted or not, I do not know.

He became something of an agnostic, in middle life, but contributed most liberally to Protestant and Catholic and Jewish charities and all houses of worship. My father was one of the financial founders of the beautiful little Catholic Church in the community where we had our summer home. He had many close friends among priests, clergymen and rabbis And a year or two before he died, too young, he began to swing back in his thinking. Having deeply loved his own father, he came to realize there must be an after life, for so good a man as my grandfather could not just perish like the beasts of the field. If there were an after life, then, there must be God.

My children have been permitted to select the churches to which they now belong; three are Episcopalian, and one a Presbyterian. When we moved to our present home they all attended a Congregational Sunday School. The girls were confirmed during their boarding school days.

Looking back, I regret that I have not been regular in church attendance. "I'm too tired, this is my one day to rest," I'd say those Sundays when I stayed at home. I think I was merely lazy. I am not a member of a church. I was christened by my grandfather and I have attended churches of all creeds. But this autumn I intend to become a member of the Congregational parish in our town.

If I had it to do over again, I would institute at the beginning the sweet habit of Grace before meals, the hearing of children's prayers, and the family reading aloud of the Bible. It is not enough to give children, as best you can, moral standards and a feeling of family security. I believe that my children are religious, at least two of them deeply so; and my younger son wishes to become a clergyman. I have encouraged this ambition, but not, I am afraid, by example.

I have always known the potent power of prayer. Twice in my earlier life it was said to me, by men who should know, that a child of mine must die. And I prayed to a Greater Healer that this should not be so. And it was not. Once not long since I was told there was no hope for someone very dear to me. All that night, every breath was a prayer; and even more recently I have kept vigils.

Those were not selfless prayers, of course, because there was threat of impending loss to myself. I suppose I never pray without self. I suppose I pray too often, within myself, for something I want or need. But usually the answer comes—not at once, sometimes a long time after, and often not in the manner I anticipated. Also, there are times when there is no answer, when I must tell myself there was something wrong for me in the desire, or that I did not sufficiently believe. To tell oneself "I believe" is not enough. Telling doesn't do it; you have to *be* believing, blind, unreasoning. It is not easy.

I have a picture of myself as I sincerely wish to be, but it is not my reflection. I fall too short; every day of my life I fail. I lead a simple, quiet life; yet there is confusion in it, and anxiety and little peace. I say, quite often, "all I have ever asked is peace of mind." But in my more rational moments I realize I have never earned it. You attract what you are, I daresay.

I have learned that there is strength, not your own, upon which you can draw in a crisis, without knowing how, or when, which tides you over when you are in the ultimate depths of despair. If I, or anyone else, knew consciously how to draw upon this at any time, how much happier and useful we would all be. But I don't fully know how. I know now that through religion some have learned this great simple art and have found the way to inner silence and tranquillity, which nothing from the outside, neither event nor emotion, can disturb.

Who does not wish he had his life to live over again? I do, every hour, but who can recall one day or half a century, of blind, or open-eyed, blundering? Yet it seems to me that perhaps we have our lives to live over again, that we can begin today, now, this minute. If today is better than yesterday, we are reliving, we have regained something and there must be rejoicing in Heaven.

I believe I could have made the way easier for my children had I made mine harder, in the sense that true and simple right-eousness is difficult I do not hold myself to be a good or even competent mother. I have been loving, but also lazy and impatient I have often taken the easier way.

In my books there is no autobiography, but I suppose something of myself is in all the characters, the good and the evil, the merciful and the cruel. Any one human being is capable of practically all good and all evil—restricted or determined by environment, background, and other factors. I do not know myself; who knows himself? Yet I know myself better than I know other people. Therefore, I assume that into my fiction, trivial as it is, there must have gone much of me as a mortal . . . of, that is, my capabilities or potentialities as a human being . . . for better or worse.

I believe that young people starting now to bring up families can be a power for good and for peace, the hope and light of the world, if there were a return to the old values and standards, to the religious training and undeviating faith in God.

NO ONE ESCAPES

by

George Sokolsky

George E. Sokolsky is one of the most brilliant and thought-provoking columnists of this generation. Millions read him every night in the New York Sun *and other papers He is a captivating public speaker and a man of deep religious convictions*

THE REASON SO MANY OF US CONCERN OURSELVES WITH THE question of faith these days is that so many of us have lost it. We do not search for what we know we have. We search for what is missing, even more we seek what we cannot do without.

Each generation forms the pattern of its own life, but always as a continuation of all its ancestors. We cannot escape our ancestors, any more than we can escape from memory or conscience. That is what nineteenth century materialism tried to do. It had discovered what it called "science," and it attempted to wash away all that the Western mind believed to be true and to substitute, for belief and faith, what they called knowledge

And so they developed geology and chemistry and physics and biology and out of it came thousands of miraculous things—automobiles and airplanes and submarines and automatic machinery and plastics and atomic bombs, and the myriads of commodities and services that we see about us and live by.

But in all this knowledge that flies out of every radio and is simplified so that little school children know so much more than their grandparents; in this world where time and space have lost all meaning so that we sit in New York and listen to Chiang Kai-

shek as he speaks in Chungking—in all this exaltation of the
knowledge of things, we seem to have lost knowledge of goodness.

We have become so complex that we have lost the simplicities
of respect for parents, love for children, loyalty to the family.
Surely those simple qualities have fallen by the wayside in a
world where divorce is almost as normal as marriage, where children are not ashamed to see their parents on relief, in which parents shirk the responsibility for the moral upbringing of their
children, in which education has been so secularized that it rejects
a moral social system and devotes itself purely to the cultivation of
functions rather than the ennoblement of character.

The story of King Midas comes to mind Everything he touched
turned into gold and he was the richest man in the world. But he
was also the poorest. For he had nothing but gold and therefore
he had nothing but misery.

We enjoy a plethora of things. The poorest person in this country can enjoy a movie, which Queen Victoria could not. Our children listen to the radio with a turn of the wrist but Napoleon had
no radio. High school boys and girls chase around in jalopies but
the richest man of his day, Commodore Cornelius Vanderbilt,
did not own an automobile.

I can go on and on, showing how rich in things even the poor
are in this country of a high standard of living. But is this richness
in things richness at all unless we preserve also the gains in character that come from moral law?

What is the value of manna from Heaven if the tablets of Moses,
the Ten Commandments, are broken and shattered into fragments? With all our knowledge of things, we have never improved upon that simple statement of moral law. Millions of
words are written every year and published in thousands of newspapers, magazines and books, but not a single word has been
added to the statement of the principles of living that Moses be-
quested to the human race as God's Word.

That is the amazing fact that we cannot escape Things add to
our joys and comfort but they do not improve our character nor

strengthen our faith in God. It is only moral law that builds character and supports faith. And moral law is always simple and clear and really is without doubt. *"Love thy neighbor as thyself,"* can be understood even by the most illiterate. One does not need to own a million things or a million dollars to understand that.

Possession does not provide happiness. It may even stimulate appetite for more and more and more. A new car every year. "Living up to the Joneses"—a phrase so prevalent in the gay twenties, when everybody went into a fierce competition for the possession of things. Mink coats and pearl necklaces are beautiful to look at and delightful to possess. But they do not make even the possessor happy, except perhaps for a moment.

But simple goodness does make for happiness. Look at Whistler's "Mother." She is happy, contented, at peace. And every line on her face bespeaks her goodness. She has not coveted; she has not stolen; she has not lost faith. She is respectful and commands respect. Her children honor her and she never divorced her husband, either for adultery or for "mental cruelty"—the lie invented by lawyers to smash one of the greatest agencies for moral living, the family within the home. What conclusion are we to reach about ourselves?

Happiness comes from goodness in life. Goodness is living within the moral law so clearly stated in both the Old and New Testaments. Possession of things may increase enjoyment of life but it does not necessarily make for happiness unless accompanied by goodness, and certainty that possession is a blessing.

And this applies to everything. Children may be taught to know more about things than Aristotle ever dreamed was possible, but if these children are not also taught the law of God, they will never know the comforts of a good and happy life. They will be without guidance. They will know no clear course. They will adhere to selfish desires without recognition of obligations and responsibilities.

Civilization cannot be measured by things. It can be measured by justice, by loving kindness, by faith.

FAITH MAKES MEN

by

Bert Kessel

A misfit and weakling in training—a youth who read the Bible in his spare time—suddenly became a battlefield hero. Bert Kessel, who led his Marine company in the invasion of Iwo Jima, tells the stirring tale of "Squeaky," one of his men, who used his faith to save lives and win a great personal victory.

MY FIRST INTRODUCTION TO PRIVATE DANNY FORREST WAS AT Hawaii. Here our Marine detachment was put through final combat training. Private Forrest, or "Squeaky" as he was called, was obviously a misfit.

As soon as Private Forrest opened his mouth all confusion regarding his nickname was cleared up. He had a falsetto voice. Squeaky was awkward, frail-looking—in fact everything a fighting Marine shouldn't be. He also bore the odious label of "eager beaver" (apple polisher).

Few Marines would have anything to do with him. When they did speak to him, it was derisively in high mock voices. Most irritating was Squeaky's effort to court everyone's favor, both enlisted men and officers. Actually this was nothing more than an earnest attempt to be friendly—to be a good fellow—but no one bothered to look at it in this light.

In typical eager fashion Private Forrest had first applied for assignment to a machine gun crew. They made him a cook. Not that Squeaky might not have made a good machine gunner. But no one wanted him in his crew.

Along with Squeaky's desire to be a good fellow, was his very devout feeling for God. Much of his free time was spent reading the Bible. He even organized a weekly prayer meeting in his tent —but few could be induced to attend. Not discouraged, Squeaky continually forced his way into "bull sessions," then would "pipe up" with some religious application to the topic of discussion. His contributions were ignored.

It was unfortunate that Squeaky tried to be such a strong disciple of the Lord in this setting, because rather than build up, he tore down the vitality of religion in the eyes of many Marines. Under a strenuous mental and physical strain Marines looked to strength for their values, and Private Forrest and his religion somehow represented weakness.

Because I felt sorry for Squeaky and had been friendly to him on several occasions, he singled me out as a special friend. One day he approached me in great agitation. With rumpled hair and his face red with suppressed anger, Squeaky was struggling to keep back the tears.

"Lieutenant Kessel," he began, "will you teach me how to fight?"

"Why?" I asked, surprised.

"Because I . . ." Then angry tears began to fall and out poured his bitter story. One of the Marines, Private Brewster, had vented his irritation against Squeaky by giving him a physical drubbing. Brewster was a tower of a man, and I judged he could probably manhandle three or four like Squeaky at one time without greatly mussing up his hair. Squeaky's determination to learn to fight and avenge his beating was absurd, but I admired his spirit.

"Look," I said to him, "it won't do any good to mix it up with Brewster again. We've got a bigger job to do than to waste time fighting each other. Why don't you try to make Brewster your friend? You two may wind up in a fox-hole together before many weeks!"

I wasn't able to discover during the next weeks if Squeaky followed my advice. None of the men knew it at this time, but we were preparing to lead the assault on Iwo Jima. Indeed, it seemed only a few days after this particular incident when my unit stormed the beaches and began to fight inch by inch for the white dust that was Iwo.

Our casualties were terrific. My first glimpse of Squeaky amid the death and bloodshed was when he hurried by fastened to one end of a stretcher. His duties as a cook were so limited that he was doubling with the stretcher crew.

And casualties among stretcher bearers were especially high. Yet here was Squeaky, the so-called weakling, jumping up at every chance to take the place of wounded bearers. Men who had scorned and despised him during training looked at him now with new expressions. The savage fighting was producing many surprises Several men, pillars of strength in training, had been pitiful failures under fire, while many of the "weak" ones were demonstrating high courage.

Squeaky was soon to perform even more spectacularly!

Fighting during the day was sheer carnage, but the nights in many ways were worse—because of the mental factor. For the Japs developed nasty habits of creeping furtively into our foxholes and quietly slicing up our men while they dozed.

For three nights this happened. Something had to be done. Then Squeaky chimed in his suggestion.

"Lieutenant," he said, "I can see good at night. Station me in the advance fox-hole, and I'll spot the Japs before they get a chance to sneak in on us."

"Why not!" It sounded crazy, but anything was worth a try. Squeaky wasn't much use with a gun, but good eyesight was a much better weapon than a gun at night.

But Squeaky almost didn't have a chance to show his cat's vision. That day he stopped some mortar fragments in his arm. The wound wasn't serious, but I ordered him to return to the hospital for repairs.

Night had just begun to fall when to my surprise there was Squeaky edging up to the advance fox-hole. I stopped him: "Forrest, I thought I ordered you out of action."

He displayed a bandage on his arm. "Look. Got it all fixed up."

The bandage was a sorry one. I shrugged my shoulders, concealing my admiration. The kid had real heart and I wasn't going to stop him from doing his stuff. I knew he had but one burning ambition—to show his fellow soldiers that he was every inch a Marine.

That night the Japs tried their infiltration tactics again. This time they didn't reckon with a slight, insignificant-looking Marine —with uncanny vision. The rest of us stared fixedly through the blackness, and saw nothing. Squeaky could see and did. He didn't dare speak out, but he could point. Then other Marines would blaze away with their rifles at shadowy lumps on the ground.

It was an unforgettable, eerie night. Many lives depending on the gestures of one man! Squeaky sometimes couldn't contain himself, and we could hear his excited whispers. Then suddenly it dawned on me who was with him in the fox-hole. *Private Brewster!*

The next morning we counted dead Japs all around the area. Squeaky was a real hero, although nothing in the kidding friendly tones of his new buddies revealed the admiration they felt. Brewster had his arm about Squeaky, and the shining light in Squeaky's eyes told me more than any word could.

I never found out when Squeaky slept. During the days he carried stretchers, and at night he was indefatigable on watch. Once during a daytime lull I saw him reading the Bible instead of sleeping. His face was serene, almost happy. Now if he could have held his Bible sessions I think the whole Marine detachment would have attended. To the men Squeaky's religion was the answer to his amazing stamina and courage. They found themselves turning to religion for courage and strength.

By the fifteenth day our ranks had greatly thinned. Brewster had been killed, and I could see that his death touched Squeaky deeply. The two had become very close. Then it happened.

Squeaky was out with the stretchers as usual. Suddenly a

mortar shell broke almost on top of him, and those nearby could almost feel the steel rip into flesh as Squeaky doubled up. Quickly he was placed on a stretcher, alive, but his stomach filled with mortar fragments. As Squeaky was carried away, his buddies looked on with blank, inscrutable expressions—mute testimony to their inner emotions. I had a lump in my throat the size of a melon.

At the end of the campaign I tallied up our losses. Of the original 260 men in my company who stormed the beaches the first day, about forty were left.

Several weeks later I received a letter from Squeaky. With much relief I read that he was out of danger. After reviewing his Iwo experiences, "a lifetime rolled into a few days," he called it, he asked about many of his buddies.

"In a way I am grateful to the Iwo campaign even though it was agony for us and death for so many swell guys," he wrote. "I found something there I had been looking for all my life."

I knew what he meant.

Squeaky's only request was that I send him his Bible and prayer material. As I fingered his religious possessions I thought of many things . . . his pitiful attempts to win friends at Hawaii . . . the amazing changes in so many men once they were under fire . . . the power of Squeaky's religion . . . the leadership it gave him. Many Marines had turned to religion on Iwo—in fear and desperation. Squeaky already had his "inner strength" when he arrived.

When I saw Squeaky praying he seemed to be thanking God for something already received. There was a great difference.

IS A.A. FOR ALCOHOLICS ONLY?

by

Bill ———

*Bill —— learned to drink during the first World
War, only to discover years later that he could not
trust himself not to drink. Pronounced incurable
by one authority on alcoholism, he was told that
recovery might be achieved through spiritual
means. Bill, an agnostic, rebelled. But finally realizing his hopeless condition, he said to himself,
"At last I'm ready to try anything. If there is a God,
will He show Himself?" This was the beginning of
Alcoholics Anonymous—*
For God did answer.

OUR MOST ENTHUSIASTIC FRIENDS THINK ALCOHOLICS ANONY-
mous is a modern miracle. So they ask, "Why can't A.A. principles
be applied to any personal problem?

"The world of today is a problem world because it is full of
problem people. We are now on the greatest emotional bender
of all time; practically no one of us is free from the tightening
coils of insecurity, fear, resentment and avarice. If A.A. can
revive an alcoholic by removing these paralyzing liabilities from
him, it must be strong medicine. Perhaps the rest of us could use
the same prescription."

Not being reformers, not representing any particular sectarian
or medical point of view, we A.A.'s can only tell the story of

[132]

what has happened to us and suggest the simple (but not easy) principles upon which, as ex-drinkers, our very lives now depend.

Fifty thousand alcoholics—the men and women members of A.A.—have found release from their fatal compulsion to drink. Each month two thousand more set foot on the A A. highroad to freedom from obsession; an obsession so subtly powerful that once engulfed, few alcoholics down the centuries have ever survived. We alcoholics have always been the despairs of society and, as our lives became totally unmanageable, we despair of ourselves. Obsession is the word for it.

But now, largely through A.A., this impossible soul sickness is being banished. Each recovered alcoholic carries his tale to the next. In a brief dozen years the A.A. message spread, chain letter fashion, over the United States, Canada, and a dozen foreign lands. Obsession is being exorcised wholesale.

What then, is this message whose power can restore to the alcoholic his sanity and thenceforth enable him to live soberly, happily, and usefully in a very confused world? The A.A. Recovery Program relates it as follows:

1. We admitted we were powerless over alcohol—that our lives had become unmanageable
2. Came to believe that a Power greater than ourselves could restore us to sanity.
3. Made a decision to turn our will and our lives over to the care of God *as we understand Him.*
4. Made a searching and fearless moral inventory of ourselves.
5. Admitted to God, to ourselves, and to another human being the exact nature of our wrongs.
6. Were entirely ready to have God remove all these defects of character.
7. Humbly asked Him to remove our shortcomings.
8. Made a list of all persons we had harmed, and became willing to make amends to them all.
9. Made direct amends to such people wherever possible, except when to do so would injure them or others.

10. Continued to take personal inventory and when we were wrong promptly admitted it.

11. We sought through prayer and meditation to improve our conscious contact with God *as we understand Him*, praying only for knowledge of His will for us and the power to carry it out.

12. Having had a spiritual awakening as the result of these steps we tried to carry this message to alcoholics and to practice these principles in all our affairs.

Simple, these principles, yet a large order indeed. When one tries to apply them he is bound to collide with a most heavy obstacle. That obstacle is one's own pride.

Who, for example, cares to admit complete defeat? Who wishes to admit to himself and others his serious defects of character? Who relishes forgiving his enemies and making amends to people he has harmed? Who would like to give freely of himself without ever demanding reward? How many can really bow before the "God of their own understanding" in real faith that He will do for them what they cannot do for themselves?

Yet A A.'s find that if we go "all out" in daily practice of our "12 Steps" we soon commence to live in a new, unbelievable world. Our pride yields to humility and our cynicism to faith. We begin to know serenity. We learn enough of patience, tolerance, honesty and service to subdue our former masters—insecurity, resentment and unsatisfied dreams of power. We find that God can be relied upon; that our strength can come out of weakness; that perhaps only those who have tasted the fruits of dependence upon a Higher Power can understand the true meaning of personal liberty, freedom of the human spirit.

For us of A.A. these are not theories; they are the prime facts of our very existence. The average A.A. member feels that he deserves little personal credit for his new way of life. He knows he might never have achieved enough humility to find God unless he had been beaten to his knees by alcohol. He was once that egocentric, but in the end it had to be God—*or else!*

Yet we of A.A. cannot but feel that great things certainly await those who will earnestly try our "12 Steps" substituting their own distressing problems for that of alcohol. Nor do we think everyone needs be so completely beaten as we were. To us, Grace is an Infinite Abundance which surely can be shared by all who will renounce their former selves enough to truly seek it out. We often feel like shouting this ancient charter of man's liberation from the rooftops of thousands of our homes—A.A. homes that would never have been, but for the Grace of God *

THE 24-HOUR PLAN

Any drunk, no matter how badly off, can go twenty-four hours without a drink, if he has half a desire to get well. Tomorrow's another matter. "Just today I'll stay sober with the help of God, if I never do another thing "

Today and how we live it, that's what matters and what adds up. Most A.A.'s need this phrase only in the early stages of their battle with the bottle. (There are some who say softly: "I've been dry two thousand and four days!")

Perhaps you can use that 24-hour plan. Others have—on love affairs—on gambling—on cigarettes—on savings—even on putting up with mother-in-law.

It works.

* Further information on the program of recovery of Alcoholics Anonymous may be obtained by writing to A A. Central Office, P O. Box 459, Grand Central Annex, New York 17, N. Y. There are no dues or fees, no alliance with any sect, denomination, politics, organization or institution.

Handicaps Can Become Assets

FAITH AND WORK CAN MAKE A MIRACLE

by

Alfred P. Haake

Can you imagine a stuttering boy developing into one of America's most sought after speakers? Dr. Alfred P. Haake, mayor of the city of Park Ridge, Illinois, tells his own personal experience in overcoming a serious personal handicap.

ONE IS NATURALLY RETICENT ABOUT RELATING HIS PERSONAL experience to demonstrate a truth, and I have always felt a little uneasy about folks who recited so easily and glibly about the power of "grace" in their lives.

But I do know something of the power which can flow through even the poorest vehicle to bless those who invoke it humbly and prayerfully. God cannot be commanded. But He can be asked. When, somehow, we adapt ourselves properly to the laws by which He rules the universe, we can bring about within ourselves changes that seem miraculous.

As a boy I could scarcely talk. I stuttered so badly that I did not recite in school. I wrote my lessons on paper or on the black-board. I was underweight, extremely nervous, oversensitive and overactive. When I played ball with the other boys they some-times called me out when I was actually safe, just to hear me sputter. I knew what I wanted to tell them, but it just piled up below my throat and left me mute. I think I can understand the agony of the cripple who is made the butt of jokes by unthinking or cruel pranksters.

One Sunday afternoon I went to a meeting in the Central Y.M.C.A. on LaSalle Street in Chicago, to hear Senator Albert J. Beveridge of Indiana. He talked to the boys about the power of God and the help He gives to those who have faith in Him. I can still close my eyes and see the Senator standing there, with his finger pointing straight at me, as he said to us, "Young man, there isn't a thing in the world you can't do, if you believe you can."

Somehow it seemed he meant that especially for me For the first time I believed I might get rid of the handicap that made life so miserable for me. I told my mother about the meeting and the newly born hope that some day I might talk to people the way Beveridge had talked to me.

She was a wise and wonderful woman, my mother! She knew something of the heartbreaks that come from overexpectations in a world that takes more joy in pulling down than it does in building up. And she patted my head gently as she said to me, "Be patient, my son. All in good time! We do not always understand the ways of God, but if we have faith and just never stop trying, some of our dreams are bound to come true."

I prayed that night when I went to bed. It was wonderful to know that God could understand the prayer I sent up without saying a word For the first time in my life I felt able to convey my thoughts and yearnings without stumbling over the ideas that cried for expression. I felt then, and I still believe now, that my petition went straight to the heart of God.

The next day did not see the kind of miracle that I might have welcomed. I still stuttered so badly that I could not talk, and the boys and girls laughed at me when I made another attempt to recite in class. But, this time I did not sit down entirely defeated. In the cavern of my chair and desk I huddled as by habit, but some of the faith I had felt the day before still remained. It was mixed with resentment and defiance, but through it I heard again the words of my mother. Yes, I could be patient. I must give God time to do this thing for me.

I read about a Greek by the name of Demosthenes who was said to have overcome an impediment in speech by talking with stones in his mouth. I thought to myself, "If he could do it, why not I?" So I went down to the beach of Lake Michigan, picked up a handful of pebbles, washed them in the ripplets that came up on the shore, filled my mouth with them and tried to talk. It did not work and I spit out the stones in disgust. I tried again, this time with fewer stones, and again and again and again. At last I literally fell on my knees in exhaustion and cried "Please God, let me talk."

I think God must have listened to my unspoken words, and known the utter pain and hunger in my heart, for as I knelt a calm came over me and I remembered the words of my mother. "Be patient, my son . . . we do not always understand the ways of God . . . never stop trying . . . dreams come true."

There followed years of trying Somewhere in Revelations I read, "He that overcometh shall inherit all things, and I will be his God, and he shall be my son." And now I knew that if I would continue unshaken in my faith and never stop trying, for that is what unshaken faith means, the day would come when my dream came true.

If, today, you went down to the shore of Lake Michigan at what used to be called Diversey Beach before the turn of the century, you would still see the waves rolling up in protest over the speeches delivered there by me so many years ago.

Words began to come, whole sentences formed in my throat and then I was reciting in high school. Leaving high school at the end of my second year, I went to work with a wholesale crockery house. I had worked before that, but it was in a factory where I simply obeyed the orders of a foreman without having or even being invited to talk back. Now I could carry on conversations, not without halting, but still conversations. And I thanked God nightly for the progress I was making.

I heard of a man who taught public speaking and went to him for help. He showed me how to articulate, to form my words and sentences and phrases at the lips. The vocal chords, he told me, were there to produce the sounds, the cavity in the mouth to enlarge the tones, the teeth to serve as sounding board and the lips to control and fashion these sounds into words and phrases.

The time came when I made a public speech. Carefully written and memorized, it carried from my heart a message that had been long in forming. I don't know who was most surprised, the audience or myself, but that speech was spoken without a single halt. There were spots where I had to wait a bit, or slow down, but I went through with the thread unbroken. From then on I sought every possible opportunity to make speeches.

There were times when courage ebbed, but always faith brought me back to the task I had assumed. My life literally became a prayer and I learned to throw myself with utter abandon into any work I undertook. In my freshman year at the University of Wisconsin, an experience delayed for eight years because of having to work for funds to get started, I was given opportunity to preach in a little country church in a nearby village. This virgin effort brought such a degree of elation and confidence that others followed and I actually preached my way through college After graduation I became a member of the university faculty and later added to my income by lecturing for the Extension Division of the university.

The time has now come when I depend largely upon public speaking for my livelihood and the greatest joy in my experiences is the ecstasy of bringing hope and inspiration to others. What was once a painful handicap has become my principal earning asset. The budding faith that began with the long finger of a United States Senator pointed at me one Sunday afternoon and the quiet assurance of a wonderful mother so many years ago, has grown into an unalterable conviction that the power of God is available to those who pray for it and are willing to risk their lives on it.

WHEN IS A MAN HELPLESS?

by

Len LeSourd

The power of a simple letter at the right time can never be overestimated Notes of hope and cheer to shut-ins and to the discouraged may help save someone's reason—change a person's despair to happiness Read what letters did for the "hopeless" case of Sergeant Gerber Schafer.

IT WAS MIDNIGHT AND THE PHONE WAS RINGING.

It was ringing in a hospital room where one light glowed softly, and where a man lay almost helpless in bed—dead from the neck down—and blind.

Gerber D. Schafer, disabled veteran of World War I, had spent twenty-four years in hospitals, flat on his back unable to move a muscle below his chin. The past fifteen have been in this same room of the St. Joseph's Hospital, Reading, Pennsylvania!

After the first ring, a nurse arose from out of the shadows, picked up the receiver and held it to Schafer's head. Other patients were asleep, but Gerber was awake—and alert. Telephone calls at this hour were commonplace.

"Hello Gerb. This is Dr. Chambers," said an urgent voice. "We'd better get Mr. Stone off to Boston tomorrow. Can't postpone the operation any longer."

Gerber's face furrowed into lines of concentration—like those of a business executive about to close a big deal. "It's all set, Doc.

[143]

Money's in the bank. Can you get him on the morning plane?"

"Yes, but I'll need money for expenses."

"Got that arranged too. Judge Melton's wife has been taking dictation for me lately, and she said she'd bring the money to you at the airport. I'll also notify the surgeon in Boston when Mr. Stone will arrive so that an ambulance will be waiting."

The nurse, who had been listening with interest and approval, hung up the receiver. Then she sighed at the realization that it would take another hour to get the Sergeant to go to sleep. She and two other nurses who attended Schafer were always torn between their admiration for his great charitable work and their professional concern that he overtire himself.

Although restricted to talking, listening, and thinking, Schafer began his working day at 6 A.M. and ended it usually some nineteen hours later at 1 A.M. During this time he entertained a steady stream of visitors, engineered fund-raising projects, served as a Reading "information bureau," dictated to his volunteer secretaries and generally performed the duties of a corporation head.

After his telephone conversation, Sergeant Schafer closed his eyes for a moment. "Dear God," he said, "thank you for giving me this chance to help another shut-in."

This particular case had been very important to Schafer. Mr. Stone badly needed a spinal operation to restore the use of his legs. He had no money. Hearing of his situation, Gerber had taken swift action. Telephone calls were made and letters written to influential people—friends of Gerber's. Soon money was raised to pay all operation expenses. The right surgeon was also found who diagnosed the trouble and predicted that if the operation was performed quickly the patient would walk again.

Today, thanks mainly to Sergeant Schafer, Mr. Stone walks.

Today, thanks to Reading's most active citizen, hospitals have new operating equipment, an ex-convict has started his own business and become a fine citizen, many shut-in invalids are earners and doers—the list goes on and on.

"The days just aren't long enough to get everything done,"

Gerb admitted to one visitor. But they are too long to suit his nurses who have had to slow him down.

New York Columnist Charles B. Driscoll, who became a great admirer of Schafer's, wrote once that if he had a disturbing problem and wanted someone's keen insight, he would seek out Gerb Schafer. "He would think about it in a simple direct way," wrote Driscoll. "Lying on his back year after year, Gerber has drifted closer and closer to Truth—and God."

But there was a time when Sergeant Schafer's spirit was as crushed and useless as his body. What made the change? Letters.

Ten minutes of one's time plus a three cent stamp. This multiplied many times rescued Schafer.

During World War I, Gerber Schafer, handsome, well-built, with steel trap nerves, had enlisted in the Air Corps. A forced landing left him badly bruised. Then came a series of operations on his back, but one by one his joints stiffened up. "Sarge," said the doctor one day, "you might as well face the facts . . ."

The rest of the words trailed off. Blackness, utter despair settled over Gerber.

"I cried out to God in my agony," Gerber stated. "I asked Him why I should live—helpless, hopeless, a nuisance to society. The pain was unbearable. I never slept over two hours a night. If I could have moved my hand enough to get at those drugs in my table drawer . . ."

Gerber's relatives and friends did what they could to help. They remembered a radio character named Cheerio who devoted some of his air time to recognition of shut-ins. Cheerio was asked if he would mention Gerber on the August 21st program. This was Schafer's birthday.

Cheerio (real name Charles K. Fields) told his coast-to-coast listeners about Gerber Schafer, who faced a lifetime on his back. Would those listening drop him a line of encouragement? Cheerio ended his program with this Bible quote· "God Whose I am and Whom I serve."

Gerber listened to the broadcast numbly, bitterly. He didn't want pity. "But I couldn't get that quote out of any mind," he revealed. "I had never served God. Now it was too late."

Then the letters and cards began to pour in from sympathetic people. They had to be answered. "I was still too miserable to care very much," Gerb revealed, "but I dictated some kind of reply." As people kept writing, Schafer kept on answering, hardly aware that an interest in these letters was slowly nibbling away at his apathy.

One day Gerb received a letter telling of a colored boy, paralyzed, who needed a motorized wheel chair. The lad wanted to sell newspapers

Schafer's heart was drawn to the youngster. Here was another cripple yearning for an outlet for his energies.

The fact that the boy's hobby was collecting stamps gave him an idea. Stamp dealers paid money for cancelled stamps in bulk quantities on the chance that a few valuable ones are among the thousands. Well, he had a long list of friends. He also had a telephone. Sergeant Schafer went to work.

Letters were written to friends asking for stamps. Advertisements were inserted in local newspapers—and on the radio. Everywhere the call was for stamps—stamps to give a crippled boy a chance in life.

Result· close to a million stamps flooded the hospital. More than enough to provided for a motorized wheel chair when turned into their cash value. Even more important—Sergeant Schafer awoke to the fact that he had a career before him—a demanding, full-time, exhausting career. With pension and insurance providing basic living expenses, he could concentrate entirely on raising money for worthy causes.

"It's quite a discovery—finding that real happiness comes from giving instead of receiving," he said "I knew then that God had use for everyone in this world. If anyone should ever doubt this, have 'em take a look at me."

YOU'LL GET
WHAT YOU ASK FOR!

by

Lucius Humphrey

Totally deaf as a boy, Lucius Humphrey was inspired with a faith that one day he would hear again. And the morning came when he heard his mother's laughter. Since then Mr. Humphrey has become the spiritual monitor of hundreds of important and successful people. He is author of It Shall Be Done Unto You.

"I DO NOT BELIEVE IN MIRACLES—I HAVE SEEN TOO MANY OF them "

This bit of cleverness of Oscar Wilde's is not amusing to me but true I deal so constantly in miracles that I *know* them to be the results of spiritual laws which are as relentless and as beneficial (according to how they are used) as natural laws.

"According to thy faith it shall be done unto you." That's all.

If you ask with any doubt whatsoever, you will not get your request, or your prayer will be only partially answered "according to thy faith." Jesus said, "Whatsoever ye shall ask in prayer, believing ye shall receive." And again "Jesus said unto him, 'Receive thy sight; thy faith hath made thee whole.' "

If then, you are not receiving "miraculous" answers to your prayers, you are not believing . . . believing that what you ask for you will receive . . . believing in the Will of God and that your prayer is in accord with His will, and that you will use it for His Holy Purpose.

People ask me endlessly how I came to have such faith. When I was a small boy, I went totally deaf through scarlet fever. My mother, however, refused to accept this deafness as final. "If you and I pray with all our hearts," she insisted, "your hearing will be perfect."

Every night she'd write on our talk-pad, "Remember, Lucius, in the morning you will hear."

That sent me to sleep believing. And the morning came when I heard her laughter. . . . Within a few months we needed no scribbled notes between us. I have never worn a hearing aid, have never since had pain, and unless I'm feeling ill or very tired, I have never had the slightest difficulty hearing.

But that was not all "God has given you your hearing through prayer," my mother told me. "See to it you listen . . . *to help Him.*"

Since this miracle of prayer I have spent much of my life listening to the troubles and confusions of others. If I have helped to bring them any peace and success through the Word, I have only tried to do with all my might what all of us, who have had prayers answered, must do to keep open the way for receiving further benefits.

People come to me with a thousand perplexities—and don't know the first thing about praying. It is all there in the Bible—in the words of Christ—all the do's and don't's that we must each strive to put into practice. I suggest that you read and learn as you grow; put into action within your powers Learn to give to the God you are asking from—give double and triple and ten times—of money, of time and of love.

It is how you use what you possess that counts. "There is no man that hath left *house* or parents or brethren or wife or children for the kingdom of God's sake *who shall not receive manifold more in this present time,* and in the world to come life everlasting." *In this present time!* What you give you get many times over if it is for God's sake. He does not want you to cling to your riches—or for them to come first, or for you to get them at anyone's expense, or use them ill. But who, looking at the wild abundance of the World He created, can doubt abundance for all?

I am reminded of two brothers who came to me for help. They were very close in age, well-to-do, of good family and personable. George from earliest age was popular, handsome, successful in all he did, keen and full of the joy of life. He came to me first because of girl trouble, and I was able to straighten him out.

Then he told me of his brother, Ted, whom he adored. Ted was far from handsome and lately far from well. He had always "played second fiddle" to George. He passed in school when George copped top honors. He got hurt in sports although he had ability enough, while George was a football hero in college. He had gotten a good job in a bank, but George went out and made a name for himself at six times the money.

The two brothers were very close and all had remained harmonious until Ted's health began to fail George was engaged to be married—brilliantly married to the girl he adored. Ted too had met the "one-and-only" girl, but she was only "fond" of him. This last blow was too much for Ted. He slowly began to lose his grip, his health and now . . . now George knew for a fact that Ted was contemplating suicide.

"Mr. Humphrey," George asked earnestly, "could you . . . would you somehow manage to see Ted and save him?"

So George and I fixed up a little plot whereby I would arrange to see Ted without seeming to be in any way concerned about his affairs. I prayed for guidance in my efforts to help the young man. As if in answer—almost like a miracle—Ted stopped in to see me, of his own accord.

His eyes were rimmed with worry, fatigue and despair. Ill-at-ease, he avoided the issue at first, but soon the whole story began to tumble out. Then as a climax he reached into his pocket, pulled out a small packet and placed it on the table before me.

It was a packet of poison!

Before I could say anything he rushed to tell me that he definitely "was not very religious and never had been."

"Well, I am," I smiled. "And I believe. How about my challenge?"

Several minutes later he began to show interest and soon had agreed to give my way a full trial.

"You admit your outlook has been pretty dark," I said.

"Darker than you'll ever know!"

"The definition of darkness is lack of light," I replied. "How about letting the light in?

"Start out," I continued, "with this simple statement. 'Let there be understanding and satisfaction in all that I am and do.' I want you to say that and promise me to repeat that ten times this afternoon and ten times before sleeping and ten times on waking. Then come to see me—lunch with me tomorrow."

There was a broad smile on Ted's face when he walked in to have lunch with me the next day. I knew God was answering my prayer and that my work with this boy would be good.

I explained to him that his own mind had accepted inferiority —that he had always expected George to shine and George had . . . so more power to him. But George had no copyright on personality. There is abundance of success and popularity for those who know how to take it and use it.

But "Be ye transformed by the renewing of your mind." He and I had a job to do to renew his mind and bring it into the light of ever-loving God.

That was in the spring. By mid-summer he had been made manager of a branch of his firm (he is now vice-president, co-owner of two other businesses, and is known as one of the most generous and public spirited men in his State). By fall the girl he cared for broke off her engagement to another and chose Ted to help her manage a big charity drive for a hospital. They were married the next June—and they have built a hospital themselves in the country for crippled children.

Miracles! Yes. But "Be ye transformed by the renewing of your mind" is not a mystical saying. It is a spiritual and holy science. Anyone who will ask and ask rightly; who will exercise control of his thinking and practice his positive faith, shall arrive not only at the place he has asked for, but will get more than full measure, pressed down and running over.

HOW TO ACQUIRE
FAITH

by

Dr. Smiley Blanton

Dr. Blanton is an eminent psychiatrist whose training included the greatest universities of Europe. He is one of the pioneers in the working partnership of religion and psychiatry. He understands people, and his wise and kindly insight will help you.

MOST PEOPLE CRAWL THROUGH LIFE ON HANDS AND KNEES. THEY have no faith to sustain themselves, to give them confidence in other people or trust in the Creator.

The spirit in them to do—to live to the full—repeats continuously, like the ticking of the clock: "I should have done . . . I should have done . . . I should have done. . . ."

"But you have not," says the sum of their accomplishments, "and now it is too late."

Too late, indeed? It is never too late through faith to tap the reserves of strength that are forever accumulating deep in everyone; never too late through faith to find the sources of power which give men courage, never too late to acquire faith in one's self, and above all, faith in other people, in other causes, other ideals With this faith, people very often do the impossible.

Without faith to rise up and carry on, life is empty. To some people even the void of death seems more desirable, for one cannot be physically or mentally healthy without faith. If you believe in nothing, why make the sacrifices for others? Why endure pain and hardship?

Lack of faith, or loss of it, can also mean the end of even life itself.

Recently I saw a woman who was recovering satisfactorily from a major operation. She thought her marriage had been happy, but about a week after the operation her husband came to the hospital and told her he wanted a divorce. Suddenly there was nothing left for the woman to believe in, life collapsed with a black crash. She began to run a temperature, and refused to eat. In a few days she became unconscious, and died.

No physical reason for her death could be discovered. But her faith had been destroyed, and life was not worth the effort of living without it.

Lack of faith is particularly noticeable in young people, the very ones who should have the most enthusiasm for life. Some were unable to compete with older brothers and sisters and with adults, and their profound sense of failure crushed faith in their own abilities. Other children were brought up in loveless homes where parents bickered continuously, and anxieties and a sense of insecurity developed where faith should have been. In adulthood these attitudes have sunk more deeply into their minds, manifesting themselves in lack of belief in friends and in the ideals which make life worthwhile.

But some adults fail to understand the cause of their inability to acquire faith. Speak to them about it, and they will give you a multitude of reasons other than the true one. They alibi that they lost their jobs because their work was unappreciated and they were not treated fairly. Actually they might have been inefficient.

Besides such self-deception, another barrier to acquiring faith is refusal to accept suggestions and the feeling that other people can't be "trusted." Naturally, one must beware of well-wishers, but most people who refuse to take any advice at all are morbidly obstinate. Their minds are closed and their hearts are hardened even to the suggestions of people who like them and who have their best interests at heart.

The third barrier to faith is the refusal to accept help, a feeling that you can and must do everything yourself. Persons with this difficulty cannot delegate authority, for they feel no one can do the job as well as themselves; they are so self-centered that they cannot believe in any power or ideal above and beyond themselves. They refuse to admit that they need the help of friends, doctor, minister, or even God.

How can these barriers of faith be hurdled? In difficult cases, a very effective method is the combination treatment of psychological medicine and religious teaching. Psychological medicine is often necessary first to break down the barriers so that religious faith may be developed.

But many people can help themselves to faith through self-examination. Make a habit of spending some time by yourself every day, of relaxing in an easy chair, or on a couch, where the cares and multiple little pinpricks of life can't take your attention, where the telephone can't call you and the radio can't make you tense with the latest news. Then think about yourself—honestly. Let your intelligence melt away the barriers to faith—the self-deception which says that bad fortune was never your fault, the negative attitude which prevents you from taking any suggestions from other people, and the self-sufficiency which drives you to try to do everything yourself.

Then, when you realize these barriers to faith, and these mental attitudes which get you flustered with life, relax even more—even beyond thinking. Slip into that thoughtless other world of reverie where lies the power to fortify you for the tasks of tomorrow.

Rebirth of faith comes to us only if we find the courage for self-examination. The vision of our own deeper selves is purely personal, but there is a yearning in all of us to think that we are newborn into a world of fresh opportunity. And new life, in a new world, can come to you—for the impulse to have it is as old as man, and as persistent.

FOUR KEYS TO FAITH

1. Neither physical nor mental health is possible without faith

—faith not only in ourselves, but also in ideals above and beyond us.

2. Through faith, it is never too late to tap the reservoirs of strength forever accumulating in each and every one of us.

3 You can acquire faith if you lay aside the cares of life, each day in a quiet hour of relaxation and self-examination dispel the barriers of self-deception and let your deeper creative forces restore you.

4. In difficult cases faith can be restored through psychological medicine and religious teaching.

DISASTER CAN LEAD
TO VICTORY

by

Harold Russell

*When the shattering blast of a TNT block
blew off his hands, the paratrooper had moaned,
"There goes the great Russell." But how wrong!
For scorning the use of artificial hands, Harold
Russell mastered the art of using hooks . . . so well
in fact that Hollywood picked him for the role of
Homer Parrish in the unforgettable film* The Best
Years of Our Lives. *Russell's acting in this picture
won him two Academy Awards and national ac-
claim for his courage in overcoming a serious handicap.*

IT SOMETIMES TAKES COLD, BLACK DISASTER TO INSPIRE ONE TO
achieve the heights of success.

But for my accident I would now be back at my pre-war job as
butcher. Instead, I have been in motion pictures, on the radio,
subject of magazine articles—but best of all, I have had a chance
to show other disabled veterans like myself that it is possible to
bounce back from utter despair to undreamed of success and happiness.

On that black June day in 1944 when I lay on a hospital bed,
looking down at two big bandages where my hands used to be, I
frankly thought it meant the end of useful living for me. What
can I do now, I asked myself bitterly? Probably just live out my
years on an Army pension.

This self-pity and despair didn't last very long though. There is something in most people that won't let them take defeat lying down. Call it anything you like, but to me it is *faith—faith* in God and in myself, *faith* that I can always rise from every setback. A man is licked without this.

At Walter Reed Hospital there was no funeral atmosphere. Nobody pitied himself or anyone else. A guy with both legs gone was called "Shorty," a man with but one leg, "Limpy;" and a soldier with only one arm, "Paperhanger." As for me—I was "Hooks." This may sound grim, but we had to develop a sense of humor, and this was the best way to do it.

My first reaction to the hooks, which were to serve as my hands, was one of dismay. The first day I tried them on, it was worse—it was torture. Unable to make them do anything, I was ready to give up. But the next day I tried again—and kept on trying until I made them work.

My first experiences out of the hospital were also trying ones. Those I met with a sense of humor were most helpful. Take the little old lady to whom I sold meat before the war. When she saw me, she broke out with "Oh, you poor boy."

Then, realizing that this was the wrong approach, she stopped and chuckled, "No wonder you lost your hands. Goodness knows you sold them to me often enough weighing my meat. They didn't belong to you anyway; I bought them many a time with my pot-roasts."

I liked that reaction—frank and sassy.

The two chaplains in our hospital were two of the finest representatives of God I have ever known. They realized that it wasn't enough to simply tell us to have faith; we had to be shown how to apply faith in overcoming our handicap. In their talks with us these chaplains had many a sharp, realistic question fired at them. They never tried to duck the "hot ones." With patience and understanding they answered everything as best they could—and their best was of real comfort to me and to the others.

There were Protestants, Catholics and Jews in our ward, but

no one was concerned as to who belonged to what church. There
may have been atheists there, but I doubt it. Certainly there were
some who had grave doubts as to God's justice in view of their
own calamity. I know I never gave up on God, and I don't believe
anyone else did either—really.

I have found that you can't tell how religious a man is by what
he says, or does.

Before my accident I recall during our combat training that religion never showed much *on* the surface, but was very much
there *under* the surface. All of us put up a tough front. We belonged to the school of realism. War was rough, so our actions and
talk had to be rough—we figured And the paratroops, I can safely
say, were the toughest bunch of all.

One man in our company, Big Joe, was the most awesome physical specimen I have ever known. Huge in stature, a calloused
hulk of muscle, Big Joe swore furiously, drank mightily and was
ready to fight at the drop of a hat. He might have been Satan himself as far as the others were concerned, but I knew different.

On our practice jumps I sat next to Big Joe in the plane and
jumped right behind him. As the tense moment arrived just before we were to go spilling out into space, I could see Big Joe's face
relax. It grew gentle, serene, and his lips moved in a quiet prayer.
At this moment I think he felt very close to God. But once on the
ground, he was a man of fierce action again, ferocious, grim, the
Devil himself.

Not all soldiers concealed their religion with such camouflage.
I know of one soldier—we'll call him Steve—who did just the op-
posite. He was friendly, brimming with good humor, a thorough
extrovert in every sense. To appreciate this story, you must get the
picture of the inside of an Army barracks. Bunks are lined up on
either side, sometimes as many as thirty on one floor. Privacy
simply doesn't exist.

In the evening just before lights went out, there was always a
terrific hubbub . . . men coming in from pass, loud arguing, singing and constant traffic back and forth to the shower. Steve was

always right in the middle of the loudest argument or the noisiest singing—until he saw time running short. Then he would break away and hustle out of his clothes.

But just before he climbed into bed, he always knelt quietly with folded hands at the side of his bunk . . . *and prayed.*

The noise, the bright lights, the confusion never bothered him. No one ever made fun of him or kidded him for it. In fact, underneath, these hard-bitten men admired and respected him for his open faith. To them it represented real courage in the face of possible ridicule. But I actually believe that Steve never felt that he was being conspicious. To him it was the right and natural thing to do.

I mention these few experiences because I have heard so many people say that the youth of today are turning away from religion. Nothing can be farther from the truth. What many people consider irreverence on the part of youth is merely impatience—impatience with churchmen who won't take more initiative in working out some of the post-war problems.

Young Americans—especially veterans of the past war—want to see the men of God roll up their sleeves and tackle some problems like these same ex-servicemen tackled the problem, say, of demolishing an enemy pillbox. Just talk isn't enough. They want action!

My chance to act the part of Homer Parrish in *The Best Years of Our Lives* was one of the finest things that will ever happen to me. Not because it made me a Hollywood celebrity, but because it gave me a chance to show thousands of other disabled people that a handicap can give them the necessary impetus to achieve more than if their calamity had never happened.

I know this to be true with many others beside myself. A close friend of mine was a great athlete before he lost both legs. This blow changed the course of his life, and now he is a brilliant lawyer with a great future before him. He admits that but for this accident his present achievements would never have been realized.

There are hundreds, thousands of similar cases. And they were all able to rise from the depths, I feel sure, not only because they had courage, but because they also had a great source of inner power—religious faith.

Inspiration—Monday to Saturday

SINGING SAM, THE HAPPY BUS DRIVER

by

Chase Walker

The legend of Sammy, who sings to his bus passengers, greets scowls with a smile and serves as a sight seeing guide along his run, has spread not only through New York City, but throughout the whole country.

SAMMY CASCAVILLA WHEELED HIS EIGHTH AVENUE BUS UP TO the 42nd Street stop The air brakes wheezed, the doors flew open and Sammy turned to his passengers.

"Ladies first," he shouted cheerfully. "This is 42nd Street . . . the Franklin Savings Bank, Times Square, the movie center. Change for Grand Central The correct time is 11 02."

Sammy's first name is really Salvatore, but along his run from 155th Street to Abingdon Square he is known as Singing Sam, the happy bus driver.

The legend of Sammy has been growing through New York City the past few years. The Eighth Avenue Coach Corporation receives a steady stream of complimentary letters about him. One described him as "the finest chauffeur in the United States." Another wrote· "The way he puts everybody in a good humor is a revelation."

New Yorkers, hardened to scowls and curt answers from city

bus drivers, have taken Sammy into their hearts. His friends along
the route include policemen, cab drivers, peddlers, storekeepers,
and just people. Passengers have learned his schedule and will let
other buses go by so they can ride with Sammy.

After race riots in Harlem several years ago, the coach company
cautiously let their first bus proceed through the hate-infested
area. It was driven by Sammy In the colored *New York Amster-
dam Stars-News* an article titled "We Salute the White Bus
Driver for Courtesy to Our People" boosted Sammy as "the perfect race relations man."

Ministers have preached sermons around Sam, newspapers have
run features about him, radio has had him on the air several times,
and short features have appeared in numerous magazines about
the "happy bus driver." In short, Salvatore Cascavilla is a simple
man with that rare combination—a great love of people and a great
faith in God.

Sam's route north begins at Abingdon Square. As he wheels
the heavy coach through traffic he sings "I love you, I love you, la-
da-de-da," to a tune that he admits is his own. At West 18th Street
he stops for a traffic light and shouts to a fruit dealer.

"How's your sister-in-law?"

"Fine, Sammy, how are you?"

"Wonderful," Sammy warbles. The fruit dealer hands him a
pear. Sammy holds it up for his passengers to see. At 66th Street
he gives it to a cop.

In the midtown section a nervous pedestrian hesitates, then
finally dashes across the street, narrowly avoiding the bus. "I love
you, I love you," Sammy sings.

At brief intervals Sammy announces the correct time. At Columbus Circle he always notes the temperature and weather information on an advertising sign and makes an appropriate
announcement. By this time the atmosphere inside the bus re-
sembles an Elk outing.

Cheerfulness and courtesy are the rules aboard Sammy's bus.
Regardless of age, all passengers are addressed as "young lady"

or "young gentleman." "They're all wonderful," he adds. Wonderful is one of Sammy's favorite words. He puts the stress on the "won."

Personal service features Sam's relations with his riders. A typical incident occurred several years ago. It was a rainy night. Two ladies carrying luggage were standing on the corner of 12th Street and Eighth Avenue, vainly trying to flag a taxi. A bus pulled up in front of them and the doors popped open.

"Climb aboard, young ladies." The cheery voice was Sammy's.

The two ladies shook their heads. "We're waiting for a cab," they answered.

Sam was not this easily shaken off. "Going to Penn Station, aren'tcha?" They nodded. Sammy then jumped out in the rain, picked up their bags and herded them on the coach with his breezy chatter. "We'll give you better service than a cab," he promised.

During the ride uptown he entertained them with lively comments and bits of information. "Everybody has troubles these days," he said. "People has gotta be cheered up. That's my job."

At Penn Station he pulled up directly in front of the station, helped them off with their luggage, then whistled for a red cap. One of the grateful women reached in her bag for a tip.

Sam shook his head. "No, thank you, young lady. It's a service of the company. Glad to have been of help."

Why does he do it? "I don't think it's hard work," he says. "My day flies. You should see those people cheer up. Even the grouchy ones are smiling when they get off. We all have plenty of troubles, but they should be left where they belong."

"You must have a million dollars," says the girl who got on at 46th Street.

"Twenty-nine cents," Sam replies. "Wonderful."

One of the letters written to the bus company about Sammy was an especially strong tribute. "That man is truly a Christian," it read, "and a fine dispenser of Christ's teachings . . kind and courteous . . . a credit to mankind and civilization . . . my conception of what we should be to make the world a better place to live in."

Quite remarkable that a short bus ride could inspire such an eulogy. Obviously there was a deep-rooted faith, a remarkable philosophy bound up in Sammy. What was the story of his life? Before starting his afternoon run, Sammy sat down in his empty bus with a GUIDEPOSTS reporter and talked about himself.

"I came over from Italy in 1923," he began "It was my life-long dream come true Two years later I got a job running the trolley. I loved the work, but knew very little English when I started. People on my car were always asking questions and I always answered 'Yes.' It was the only word I knew, so it had to do for everything."

Sammy smiled ruefully as he recalled these early experiences. "People would get mad at me for giving them wrong answers, so I had to learn English quick. I wanted only to make people feel good.

"I met my wife, Josephine, on my Broadway trolley," he remembered with a far-away smile. "Her folks were regular riders. One night they asked me to go to 'Aida' That did it "

A slight shadow crossed his face. "Five years ago I have great troubles come into my life. My wife had bad cough so I take her to a doctor. He X-rayed her lungs. What a terrible thing she had! Very bad spot on both lungs.

"The doctor said she could not get well. I did not lose faith though. I couldn't. Finally, one doctor told me to send her to a place where the air was clean and fresh. It was the only hope. I had very little money, but the bus company said I could work double shifts.

"I fixed my wife with room at Lake Saranac, and started to drive bus day and night to pay for it. Then I learn something. When people have much trouble it is easy to be grouchy and hard to be cheerful. I wish to forget my trouble while driving my bus, so I try to smile and talk a lot. Pretty soon I find it easy to be cheerful.

"I go to Catholic Church every Sunday and pray for my Josephine. I never lose faith any time. On my bus route I learn all the churches—Catholic, Jewish, and Protestant. Then I call them off to my passengers. People should know more about churches.

"Soon I find that most people have lots of troubles More and more I try to cheer them up, make them smile. One day a lady got on my bus, sat behind me and told me all about the terrible trouble with her son. She started to cry. But not for long. I started to sing, the people on the bus began to smile and laugh, everybody was having fun   . it was a wonderful day. Pretty soon the lady stopped crying and was smiling too. 'I'm not going to be the only sad one in the bus,' she told me. That made me feel fine."

Sam looked at his watch, slipped into the driver's seat and started the engine. "Getting her warmed up," he explained.

But Sam had not finished talking. Sam is one of those who will talk to people as long as they will listen "I love children the most . . . and old folks too. They have the hardest time taking care of themselves . . . the old and the young. Mothers put their children on my bus in the morning, and I see that they get to school," he added proudly.

"My wife was away for two years. The doctor . . . he rides on my bus, you know . . . he operated on her and it was fine success. Now she is home and well."

As Sammy prepared to wheel his bus into traffic, his teeth flashed into a wide smile. "God has been very good to me. This is a wonderful world."

TRACK THIRTEEN

by

Len LeSourd

"I wouldn't trade my job for any in the world,"
says Ralston Young, Redcap No. 42 of New
York's Grand Central Terminal. This inspiring
Negro personality serves people not only by car-
rying their luggage, but also by conducting his
famous "Track Thirteen" spiritual service every
Monday, Wednesday and Friday noon.

As STATION PORTER NO. 42 PUSHED HIS EMPTY BAGGAGE CARRIER
up the ramp in Grand Central Terminal, another Redcap hailed
him

"Hello, Preacher."

Redcap No. 42 turned and smiled easily into the irreverent face
of his co-worker.

"I don't mind your calling me that," he said, "but take off the
'P' and make it 'Reacher,' will you? All I'm trying to do is reach
out a bit and help other people find themselves"

The other porter grinned back It was hard to get irritated with
this good-natured Negro.

Ralston Crosbie Young, the porter No. 42 in question, is known
to millions as Grand Central Terminal's "Most Unforgettable Redcap." A medium-sized man of forty-five, Ralston makes a career
of carrying luggage and offering comfort to the discouraged and
the bewildered. This eager disciple of God has discovered that a
busy railroad terminal is an ideal place to practice religion every
day of the week

Each Monday, Wednesday and Friday noon Ralston conducts the now famous "Track Thirteen" worship service Executives and clerks, railroad employees and officials, travelers, men and women of all walks of life gather on these days at the stroke of twelve in front of Track 13 in New York's Grand Central Terminal. Ralston then unlocks the gate and all file down to a vacant coach for a fellowship prayer meeting.

"We're just a group of people who like to talk and pray together and find a solution to our problems through Christ," Ralston explains simply.

The meetings began back in 1944 when Ralston having heard about other small prayer groups which were meeting regularly in shops, factories and offices, gathered together several interested persons.

When the *Reader's Digest* featured Ralston and his unique prayer service, men and women of faith throughout the world made a mental note to attend should they ever get to New York. But along with the cheers came the inevitable jeers. Jibes from some of his fellow workers cut deeply at first. Dislike for several of the men welled up so strongly in Ralston at times that he got down on his knees and prayed about it.

"I had to learn to love the hate right out of my system," he declared.

One Wednesday Ralston arrived at the track gate to greet several old friends, including a retired railroad official, a pastor from New Jersey and a Mr. Johnson from Pennsylvania. Then he introduced himself to three newcomers. a young blond giant who looked like he could play football for anybody's team, a slim merchant seaman, and a GUIDEPOSTS reporter.

This group—an interesting cross section of American life—filed down to an unlighted coach, which was illuminated solely by rays from the platform lights. Coach seats on both sides of the aisle were adjusted to seat seven. The atmosphere was informal, relaxed.

Ralston opened with a short prayer, calling for peace and understanding in a troubled world. Then he began the discussion by telling of an incident where he felt called on to defend the Bible before a group of his coworkers.

"I knew they were trying to put me on a spot," he said, "but I controlled myself and waited for the Lord to give me the right answer He did."

Others then joined in the discussion, eager to tell of their own special problems. As they talked each one found himself being drawn more closely to the others Barriers slip away easily somehow when people *know* they are in the presence of *Him*.

The merchant sailor was the last to join in the conversation. Shy at first, the lad soon talked freely. He had read about "Track Thirteen" while on shipboard thousands of miles away from home. Inspired by the story, he had resolved that some day he would get to New York and attend a meeting.

"Now that I've had a chance to meet with you people, I can see that 'Track Thirteen' can go on forever. On my next voyage I'm going to try and organize a meeting like this on shipboard." The young man's enthusiasm left an atmosphere of quiet elation in the coach.

The meeting then broke up. Spiritually refreshed, all started back to their normal routines, each one feeling a new strength and vigor to meet the problems of the day.

Ralston, however, was still willing to talk further about "Track Thirteen."

"Years ago," he stated to the GUIDEPOSTS reporter, "I tried everything to find happiness. Nothing lasted. Then I began to live my life for Christ. It was as simple as that. I then found the happiness I had looked for so long."

"It hasn't all been easy though," he continued. "I've made mistakes and gotten off the course many times. But just when I feel lowest, something always happens to give me a new zest for life and even more faith in God.

"Take Mr. Johnson who was here today," Ralston said. "He had a brother who was very sick. Hearing of our 'Track Thirteen' prayer fellowship, he came one day simply to pray for his brother.

"When he told us about his brother, we all prayed for him too. Then he returned for a second time, and a third. Finally, he told us that he believed our prayers were doing more good than anything else to help his brother pull through. We felt wonderful about it.

"Mr. Johnson's faith in his brother's eventual recovery grew with each visit. For a time it did seem that his brother would recover. Then suddenly he died.

"As far as Mr Johnson was concerned," Ralston went on, "that did it. He was through with us—and worse—with God. He figured that God had let him down. I felt very bad. It was just one of those things hard to understand and explain. Mr. Johnson was a fine man, but this hurt was more than he could take at that time.

"This all happened over a year ago. We didn't see Mr. Johnson again as the months went by, but we never forgot him in our prayers. Several weeks ago I was in a particularly low mood. Troubles seemed to be ganging up on me from all sides. I guess the Lord decided one Friday that I needed a special lift. That noon when I came to 'Track Thirteen' . .

There was Mr. Johnson.

"He didn't have to tell me why he had finally come back. I knew he would some day. He had found out that living a life without God is living without hope or happiness."

"Ralston," Mr. Johnson said to me later on, "I suddenly realized that all along I had been asking God to give *me* something. I had never once tried to give something to Him in return. You just can't deal with God that way."

It was time for Ralston to go back on duty. As he locked the gate and turned toward the congested station floor, a gleam of excitement and—something else—came into his eyes. "You know, Grand Central Terminal is a parish—a big one and a mighty good one. I wouldn't trade my job here for any in the world."

GOD KEEPS SCORE

by

DeWitt (Tex) Coulter

Rugged, 260-pound "Tex" Coulter, crashing football tackle from Fort Worth, Texas, won All-American honors two years in a row while playing with the great Army teams of 1944 and 1945. Now a stellar lineman for the New York Giants Professional Football Club, "Tex" discloses how faith works on the football field.

It's easy to be selfish and vain on the football field. You can read too many clippings about yourself, or let the roar of the crowd go to your head.

I know.

Sometimes I feel a special urge to show what a powerhouse of action I can be. A rock on defense, a dynamo on offense—as much a standout as a tackle in the line can be—that's for me. It's human to have such temptations, but to let them run away from you, that's bad.

When I feel these "Big Me" urges coming on, I switch my thinking quickly to the team and how we operate as a unit. Then I concentrate on doing the best job I can in the interests of the team. If I don't switch my thinking in time, sooner or later I'll make some mistake that will cost us yardage. A football eleven can have eleven All-Americans, one for every position, but if each is trying to be a star on his own, any well-trained team with moderately good players can beat the daylights out of it.

Too many people, I'm afraid, have acquired a lot of wrong ideas about professional football players. The great majority of men I know in the professional ranks represent the finest type of men. Most of us are married and live normal home lives.

As long as I have been playing, I have never heard anyone "knock" religion. A great many of them are regular church-goers. Because of the great pressure of publicity and the spotlight that is constantly focused on us, and the people who want to lionize, entertain or "treat" us, we meet up with a great many more temptations than the average person. In the face of this, amazingly few players go off the beam.

My religious thinking began in earnest back in my Fort Worth high school. I'd been brought up in a Mason's Home (an orphanage), and been given sound religious training. But at some time each man has to do some pretty straight religious thinking on his own, and figure out just where he stands in relation to God in his own way.

In my high school days, I had a friend whom I'll call Billy Jackson. He seemed to typify to me how a really religious person should act. He not only went to church regularly every Sunday, but often during the week. "My life career," he told one and all, "is devoted to religious work." He never cussed. He never allowed others to cuss in front of him if he could prevent it. He made a point of urging others to religious practice.

All this hardly won him the "most popular" label, but his fervid sincerity did command a certain amount of grudging respect. Then one night for no reason I could see, Billy went haywire. He stormed into town and proceeded to get drunk—publicly.

Naturally, this created a sensation because on top of his religious convictions, he had expressed strong anti-drinking views. Though somewhat stunned by what he had done, Billy was soon back in stride again, waging his one-man campaign against sin. But now underneath his pious manner, it was quite apparent that he wasn't happy. And it wasn't long before he veered off the beam again. These slips began to occur more and more often. This whole performance deeply disturbed me. Was it that religion couldn't help him in times of temptation—or was it that he was not sincere in religion or was practicing it as a sort of escape from himself?

We watched Billy go down and down, unable to help him. And it burned me that he did a lot of people harm, for they tied his failure and religion together in such a way as to lower their estimation of any practical value of a religious life.

But God works in a mysterious way. That seemingly bad influence of Billy's was what really started my thinking. Where did I stand myself in regard to temptation and sin?

Just why was I here on earth anyway?

I arrived at the conclusion that if I wanted eternal life in God's Plan, I would have to live in such a way as to prove that I was worthy of it.

Like all humans I am equipped with the standard faults of selfishness, vanity, and a tendency to give in to temptations. Therefore, I began to concentrate on fighting off selfishness and temptation. I have a strong belief in God and His plan—and I am convinced that it doesn't involve passive selfishness. I believe that from the moment Adam sinned against God, God decided that the earth would be a proving ground for all the people in it. In other words, *the right to an eternal, heavenly life must be earned.*

I am particularly thankful that I found the answers to my earlier confusion about God and after-life. From then on, my life had more meaning and purpose. I can now direct my energies to serving my God with the words of His Son in mind, as I explore them in the Scriptures and hear them expounded in church.

My wife and I go to church as often as we can. Whenever I need to straighten out my thinking, the quiet, restful atmosphere of the church never fails to recall to me the important things in life.

On every out-of-town trip over a weekend, the New York Giants consider the religious interests of the players as thoroughly as they do the eating and sleeping arrangements. A man is sent ahead to handle accommodations. He looks up the location of all Christian and Jewish houses of worship and gets a schedule of all services. When the men arrive in town, they are informed as to where their

particular churches are located, what time the services are held
and who the ministers are.

Football has helped teach me many lessons, one of which is that
there must be a certain amount of sacrificing in everyone's life. I
am learning to suppress my desires for personal glory for the good
of the team. I believe that this kind of sacrifice is necessary in every
form of living. It's not easy, though.

It helps me to think of life as a game with God keeping score of
every yard lost or gained. Grantland Rice expressed how I feel
about the sportsmanship of living so that I can visualize myself
playing on God's team. He said:

> *"And when the One Great Scorer*
> *Comes to write against your name,*
> *He marks not that you won or lost,*
> *But how you played the game."*

DOING THE LORD'S WORK–IN TRACK PANTS

by

Gil Dodds

Unbeaten on the track since 1943, holder of the world's indoor record for the mile run, Gil Dodds is one of the great athletic champions of this age. Gil discloses here his spiritual formula—and that of many other great athletes—which can make the difference between a good performer and a champion.

MANY PEOPLE THINK THAT RELIGION IS FOR SISSIES—AND THE weak, the sick, the aged, and the desperate. But those who take the trouble to look closely will discover that religion and faith have always produced the greatest examples of courage and heroism.

If these skeptics refuse to be impressed with the courage of our religious forefathers, however, they will be impressed by the actions and beliefs of present-day heroes on the athletic fields of America. And here is something they should know. *Many of the greatest athletes of today, champions in all fields, are deeply religious men—and pray before each contest.*

These expressions of faith by athletes do not receive space on the sports pages, hence, their admirers never discover this side of their heroes. Many athletes will not express their religious beliefs openly for fear they will seem like hypocrites. Thus, many people form the mistaken idea that all sports figures are hard-playing, hard-living men, with no interest in religion.

Gunder Hagg, one of the greatest runners in the history of track, and against whom I had the fortune to compete some years ago, always prayed before each race. During one meet in which Hagg, Bill Hulse, and myself were to run the mile, I asked Gunder with friendly interest what he prayed for.

"Gil," he said, "I was praying for all of us—you, Hulse, and myself."

"Didn't you pray that you'd win?" I asked quizzically.

He shook his head. "I just prayed that each one of us would do his best," he replied simply. The perfect answer from a great champion. Hagg then went on to win the race too.

This is only one case, but I know of many other athletes in track alone who prayed regularly before a race. Many were champions in their field, who looked to God to give them strength and that "something extra" which most champions have.

My sports philosophy is not to run with the idea of breaking a record, or even solely to win, but *to do my best*. Sports fans demand this from all contestants. Those who don't produce their best, receive a full blast of fan disapproval—and deserve it.

One of the greatest thrills in sports is to see some seemingly outclassed performer come from far behind to whip the favorite. How did he do it? By giving his best regardless of how hopeless it seemed.

The same idea holds true with religion. Christians are judged according to their effort and the good they can accomplish. Becoming a good Christian takes the same hard work that goes into training for running a race.

Sports can teach great Christian lessons. Defeat, for example, taught me the lesson that I must learn how to examine myself, find the reasons for defeat and overcome them.

Back in 1943 I was winning races consistently. Gradually the idea took root that I was good enough to produce whenever I wanted to. This attitude alone was enough to take the edge off my will to win and prepare me for a licking.

It happened at the Millrose games. Running the mile, I had

led most of the way, was in front on the home stretch, and prepared for that pleasing sensation of finish cord breaking against
my chest. Then out of nowhere came a runner to flash by and
nip me at the tape

An accident, I thought to myself, after recovering from the first
shock of surprise and dismay.

But in the next race I finished third and was beaten most of the
way. This brought me up with a jolt I took stock of myself. Then
I realized that my attitude was much to blame. I had forgotten the
Lord and was running for Gil Dodds.

Before the next race I trained carefully, with humility, praying
that I might run my best. I did and won.

This victory restored my waning confidence, but unfortunately
it also restored some of my old arrogance and conceit. It just
seemed that my other two defeats were accidents after all. The
lesson hadn't been completely learned—yet. Then came the Na-
tionals and Knights of Columbus meets, and I lost the mile in
both.

These defeats conclusively taught me one of the most important lessons I have ever learned. I can never do my best without a
proper mental attitude, and this proper mental attitude depends
on humility before God. Two Biblical passages describe this per-
fectly: "Without Me ye can do nothing," and "Whom the Lord
loveth He chasteneth."

I learned another lesson in a race I ran this past winter It was
also in the mile run. I was leading around the final turn when it
occurred to me that I might have a chance to break the record.
Excited by this thought, I put on a final spurt, but my pace became uneven and I staggered and nearly fell. Luckily, I managed
to right my stride in time to win, but this sudden vain desire to
break a record nearly cost me the race.

That night I read a passage in St. Paul's Epistle to the Hebrews
and realized how I had forgotten in the heat of the race Paul's
counsel of patience in all things.

I have found that in the Bible one can find the solution to every problem and every question about life. Yet so few search there for these answers!

All athletes have their own formulas for preparing themselves mentally for a contest. Mine is quite simple. Since the majority of track meets are in New York, I have discovered a church that holds a service each Saturday evening at six-thirty. After attending this service, I return to my room and read the Bible or simply rest and think about God. Soon I am completely filled with a quiet peace and assurance. I then see the race in its proper perspective and relative importance.

During the past few years I have had opportunities to do some student coaching. Over and over I stressed to my charges the importance of their attitude, that they should never concede defeat, that they should always do their best no matter how hopeless it seemed. Those who loafed found themselves on the sidelines during the next meet.

The rules to be followed for becoming a top athlete can be narrowed down to an essential two: First, one must develop the body. This means clean living, regular sleep, regular meals, and plenty of exercise. Smoking and drinking hurt body efficiency.

A strong body alone is not enough to make a champion. A good mind is also essential. For an athlete must be able to absorb knowledge and coaching and above all to understand the basic principles of sportsmanship. The proper mental attitude is to aim for the top, to concede victory to no one, to be equally a good winner and a good loser, and to look to God for strength and courage.

Common Ground Between Science
and Religion

THERE ARE NO ATHEISTS IN LABORATORIES

by

Gustavus J. Esselen

A research chemist, Dr. Gustavus Esselen admits that he looks at religion along scientific lines. He is convinced that religion is of vital importance today, and that science and religion are in complete harmony. Dr. Esselen is president of Gustavus J. Esselen, Inc., consulting chemists and chemical engineers, Boston, Massachusetts.

I HAVE BEEN A SCIENTIST FOR OVER THIRTY-FIVE YEARS AND HAVE yet to find one who is an atheist.

This may surprise many people who believe there is considerable conflict between science and religion. Nothing can be further from the truth. The more I learn about life and the laws that govern it, the more I realize that there has to be a Supreme Intelligence behind it all.

A lady once looked at a magnificent sunset painted by the artist Turner. After a few minutes of study she turned to the artist and remarked, "I never saw any such colors in a sunset, Mr. Turner."

Without a minute's hesitation the artist replied, "Madame, don't you wish you could?"

In the same way people look at religion from many different viewpoints. Some *can* perceive its great beauty and power. Others look at religion logically; a few are indifferent. Some even try to find its beauty but do not know how to go about it. Being a research chemist it is perhaps logical that I look at religion along scientific lines.

We know that nature is governed by law and not caprice. Likewise, we know to the exact second when the sun will rise in the morning. Still more amazing, we can figure to the fraction of a minute when eclipses of the sun will occur hundreds of years from now. Thus, I try to set up for myself a worthwhile aim in life which will be in harmony with the general plan of things as man is gradually able to unfold it.

It is often repeated that the main purpose in life is to obtain happiness. I agree, provided that the type of happiness is clearly defined. Einstein once said, "To make a goal of happiness and comfort never appealed to me; a system of ethics built on this basis would be sufficient only for a herd of cattle."

If he means mere lazy comfort, I agree with him, but if it is joy and happiness with a sense of a task well done, I think that is a goal well worth striving for. Remembering that happiness for all, as well as for one, involves the conquest of disease and improvement of social and political conditions throughout the world, we must agree that it is a worthy aim in life.

How to accomplish this? Find a job to be done, then do it to the best of your ability. This rule has been repeated many times, but then most of the really important rules of life have become hackneyed through overuse.

Today there is a great sense of urgency in the air; the failure of a single individual's contribution may affect the whole civilized world. In pre-historic times the discovery of a healing herb would benefit only a small localized group of cave dwellers, and the news would take years to spread to other tribes. A war then would involve but two segregated elements. Today the discovery of a new drug is quickly flashed around the world for the benefit of all, while the assassination of one man can throw the whole world into war.

So I now arrive at two age-old principles from a somewhat new angle. First, the Golden Rule of "do unto others as you would have them do unto you" applied not merely to personal relationships but to the greater responsibility of an individual to the world. Secondly, defining right and wrong not according to a pattern of laws laid down by men who lived centuries ago, but according to what is harmful or beneficial to the human race today.

Luther Burbank had the right idea. He once said, "If I have made any worthy contribution to the world, it is . . . that a plant born a weed does not have to remain a weed, or that a plant degenerated by conditions of nature does not have to remain degenerate."

When asked if this applied to human beings, the great botanist replied with an emphatic *yes* "Heretofore," he said, "when we found a dwarfed plant or weed or fruit that seemed to have degenerated until it was worthless, we had assumed that God meant it to remain so or it would never have reached that deplorable state So we allowed it to remain a useless thing, a parasite on life, an obnoxious, ill-smelling outcast. But I have proved the principle that there is no plant so great an outcast that it cannot with skill and care be reclaimed."

Here is a scientific principle equally dynamic in its application to plant life and human beings. Here also is an example of the close teamwork that can function between science and religion. Science starts the ball rolling with the discovery of a method of transforming plant life, religion takes the findings and uses them in the transformation of people. Broken lives can be salvaged, while the spiritless and disillusioned may be rejuvenated by a new purpose in life.

The goal of both religion and science becomes the betterment of mankind.

As a boy I believed in Santa Claus. He was a jolly, generous old fellow, who visited each home the night before Christmas and left behind generous samples of his bounty. When I grew older I still believed in Santa Claus, but he no longer was the fat fellow in a sleigh. Instead, he had become the spirit of giving, the spirit of kindness and generosity around Christmas time.

In my youth I believed in God as an all-powerful Father, who created the world and all the people in it, and who could be kindly or stern as the situation demanded. Today I still believe in God, but through science I have come to understand better how He masterminds the universe and yet provides us with the minds and abilities to work out our own destiny. To me God is an Omnipotent Force, far beyond our comprehension, who planned all this and many other things which our five limited senses do not permit us as yet to perceive.

The church is of such great importance today that its influence on the community can never be overestimated. A practical example of the value of church to community occurred not so many years ago in a small Maine factory town. The church had been closed for lack of support, and so the village life grew from bad to worse morally speaking. Finally, the situation deteriorated to the point where owners of the factory decided something had to be done. After careful study it was decided to reopen the church with plant support When this was done, the moral tone of the community immediately improved.

What actually had happened? With no religious stimulus in their lives, the people in this village not only "went to the dogs" morally and became unhappy and discontented, but the plant output actually suffered. The re-installation of the spirit of religion transformed the whole atmosphere.

It is interesting to compare the fields of religion and sciences as to adopting new ideas. Years ago the late Dr. E. E. Slosson said, "In order to introduce a new idea into the mind of man, it is generally necessary to eject an old one. All through the history of science we find that new ideas have to force their way into the common mind in disguise as if they were burglars instead of benefactors of the race." Religion too has used up centuries in throwing off old superstitions and intolerances, thus delaying the emergence of religion as the effective means of happy, abundant living.

Today most of the progress in science is the result of organized research, rather than the work of independent geniuses working alone in garret or cellar. In like manner, it will take the pooled abilities not only of persons of all religions, but also of those skilled in research in many branches of science as well, if we are to find the secret of how Man is to live peacefully with his fellow Man.

LIVING BY THE SPIRIT

by

Arthur H. Merritt

The influence of a godly Mother largely shaped
the career of one of America's greatest professional
men. Dr. Arthur H. Merritt became a widely read
scholar as well as one of our country's most distin-
guished members and leaders of the dental profes-
sion. Author, lecturer and churchman, he is past
president of both the American College of Dentists
and the American Dental Association.

I HAD THE GOOD FORTUNE TO HAVE BEEN BROUGHT UP IN A GODLY
home. My mother, who was a widow at thirty-one, with six children, of whom I was the eldest at ten, would gather that small
brood about her each morning after breakfast, and in language
more eloquent than any which I possess, would commit them to
the care of One whom she knew better than her neighbor in the
next farm house. All that I am or can ever hope to be, I owe to my
mother and to the God whom she worshiped. I wonder if any of
us can ever repay the debt we owe to our mothers? I am sure I
never can.

The church and Sunday school played almost no part in my
life during early childhood. We lived three miles from the little
church in the village with no way of getting there except we
walked or drove the farm horse. It was my mother rather than the
church that influenced me in those early days.

Later my mother moved to a nearby city. There with my
mother, two brothers and three sisters, I attended a Methodist
church.

During the winter when special services were being held, I gave myself wholly and unreservedly to the God whom I had learned to know at my mother's knee. It was to me a transforming experience. I came to know something of what St. Paul meant when he said: "If any man be in Christ, he is a new creature: old things are passed away; behold, all things are become new." It changed the whole current of my life. I began at once setting aside ten per cent of my small earnings as belonging to my Maker, and cut loose from everything that might handicap me in my new-formed purpose to "live by the faith of the Son of God." I was in dead earnest.

Soon after this I left home with no more definite purpose than that of bettering my position in life. How I was to do this I did not know. I had never before been away from home. I was lonely. I had no money, no influence, no friends to whom I might turn for advice. Somehow I felt I would be guided. Again and again I was tempted to turn back. Why I did not, I could not then have told. I know now.

I soon obtained a job as traveling salesman at which I continued for a year and a half, my income being wholly dependent upon my sales. I made it a rule to attend church wherever I happened to be, for the church, next to my mother, has been the most potent influence in my life. Since then I have been a member of seven different churches due to changes in location, including four different denominations.

Gradually as my small savings increased, the opportunity presented which made it possible for me to take up the study of a profession. This again changed the current of my life and opened to me a new world. It meant life in a great city—to me a new experience. All doubt as to what my course in life was to be disappeared. The goal was now clear and I pursued it with enthusiasm, never doubting that success would crown my efforts.

Immediately after getting settled in my new environment, I joined a church and took an active part in its services.

It was in this first city church that I met a man—about twice

my own age—who made an indelible impression upon me. He
lacked much that the world esteems great. But this he made up
by a life completely "hid with Christ in God." He was the most
Christ-like person I ever knew. For two years I roomed with him
and came to know him intimately. His affections were set on
things above. To him Christ was more real than his next door
neighbor.

To have known him I count as one of the richest blessings of
my life. It was an experience I shall never forget. Though he
passed to his reward many years ago, his photograph still occupies
an honored place in my home. He was "my most unforgettable
character." Once when I was rooming with him he suggested that
I select some verse from the Bible that I might always hold before
me as a guide to daily living. The verse I chose was: "He that saith
he abideth in Him ought himself also so to walk, even as He
walked." Throughout all the intervening years these words have
been "a lamp unto my feet and a light unto my path." They have
been my "guidepost."

Many years have passed since then. Success and honors have
come to me making possible a life of service such as I had never
dreamed of—service to my profession, my church, and to my fellowmen. At no time has there been any doubt in my mind of the
guiding care of that "divinity that shapes our ends, rough hew
them how we will." The thought that I am a "laborer together
with God," is always with me. I am in very truth, "his workman-
ship, created in Christ Jesus unto good works, which God hath
before ordained that we should walk in them." For I know that it
is only as we walk in them can the "kingdoms of this earth become the kingdoms of our Lord and his Christ."

Often during the day—in the home, on the street, in the office
—I remind myself that I belong, not to the things round and about
me, but to the God of my mother, that it is not I that achieves,
but the Spirit that worketh in me. In this way I am able to "practice the presence of God"—to live in constant companionship
with Him. To find Him I do not need to go outside myself. I have

only to remember that I am in His presence and to recall my spirit to the consciousness that wherever I am, there is God also; that no matter what the difficulties may be, "I cannot drift beyond His love and care."

On a table by my bedside are several books. Before closing my eyes in sleep, I spend a few minutes in reading and re-reading these favorites. It may be the Bible, Emerson's "The Over-Soul," or Browning's "The Guardian Angel,"—anything that meets my need at the time In this way, I shut out the noise and confusion of the day's activities and take refuge in the things of the Spirit. As I close my eyes in sleep, I repeat to myself something from the Bible—the 91st Psalm, parts of the Sermon on the Mount, the 13th of First Corinthians, or possibly some favorite poem. My last waking thought is of my oneness with the Spirit, and my first as I open my eyes on a new day.

Written in indelible letters on the tablet of my mind are these lines from Henry Drummond: "To become like Christ, is the only thing in the world worth caring for, the thing before which every ambition of man is folly and all lower achievement vain."

This is what living by the Spirit means to me.

On Making Right Decisions

TECHNIQUE FOR MAKING A DECISION

by

Roger W. Babson

Harassed by a vexing problem, unable to think and pray over it in proper surroundings, Roger Babson one week day wandered into an open church Out of this experience grew an effective technique for making good decisions. Mr. Babson, head of the Babson Institute in Wellesley, Massachusetts, is a distinguished author and an outstanding business leader.

I WAS OVER SIXTY YEARS OLD BEFORE I EVER SAT FOR A HALF-HOUR quietly alone in a church.

For some weeks I had been troubled in making a difficult decision The problem involved several people, and I wanted to be fair to all as well as to myself. It seemed impossible to find an opportunity to think and pray by myself in proper surroundings. At my office the telephone was always ringing; in my home members of my family were running about; it was winter so I could not go out into the woods by myself.

As I was passing a small Episcopal church the thought occurred to me that it might be open. If so, I would go in. The church was open and comfortable. A stream of sunlight poured in through the western windows. I sat down undisturbed in this sanctuary of peace and quiet beauty.

It took a little time for me to get acclimated to these new surroundings, but I soon did I said a little prayer asking for help in finding a solution to my difficulty. Then I waited. Gradually the factors in the situation assumed their correct proportion, and the answer began to take shape. I arrived at a clear decision! Better still, there came a confidence and courage to act upon this decision The whole experience was a revelation to me.

The success of this experience prompted me to tell my story to a group of people in my own church in Wellesley Hills, Massachusetts. For our church was one of the many closed during the week Then I suggested that it be opened during certain hours to any stranger that might be passing by. The idea struck immediate favor, and a plan was worked out to keep the church open for at least an hour every afternoon and evening.

But interested church members did not stop here. They felt that such benefits should be enjoyed by strangers and church members alike Thus, it was proposed that laymen and laywomen be charged with the responsibility of opening the church during these hours. In this way sixty or more busy church members would have a chance to spend at least an hour a month in the quiet solitude of the church

The truth is that not only are most Protestant churches closed during the week, but their ministers are placing no emphasis on what it means to *sit by one's self in quiet prayer and meditation in a church edifice.* Church officers are apt to lack interest because keeping the church open increases the heating expense and janitor service.

It is my sincere belief that any church which adopts a policy of keeping the church open would have no trouble in raising money for heating from people who have benefited from the privilege of quiet meditation. One reason why some churches have so much difficulty in raising money is because the people to whom they go for money have received so little concrete benefit from the institution.

The first step toward profiting from meditation alone in a church is to leave all extraneous thoughts at the door. The church

is no place in which to worry. The real purpose of quiet meditation is to clear the mind of these cares, to refresh the soul, and to
get into a mental and spiritual state where right solutions will
automatically come to us.

Once when going to have an operation, I remember telling the
doctor of my fear of taking ether. "Many patients have the same
fears," he replied. "Just don't try to *breathe in* the ether Simply
blow out the air already in your lungs." It worked like a charm.

For weeks now you may have been worrying over some problem. Perhaps you have been putting the cart before the horse. Instead of "breathing in" more worries, the Church can help you
blow them out! Then a solution to your problem can *come in!*

When I first enter the church for meditation, it sometimes is
from a sense of duty I feel fidgety and out of place. I am in a
hurry to "pay my pence" and go about my business. But slowly
repose and serenity come to me—whether I be in a great cathedral
or a humble country-meeting house. This is especially true if the
building is historic, but if not I think of the age of the Church
for which it stands. The Church is the oldest organization in every
community. This thought alone gives me calmness and poise.

I enter thinking of some special man or woman, but I leave
thinking of manhood and womanhood. I enter thinking of specific things like a product or house, but I leave thinking of an industry or home The Church teaches me to think more of the
larger things and less of the unimportant things.

Meditation in a church broadens my horizon and makes me
think of others in an unselfish and constructive way.

One friend of mine, who has kept our church open for an hour
each month for years now, has had but one caller. This caller—
although a stranger—happened to work in the same factory with
my friend! As a result of this meeting my friend ever since has
each day invited to lunch one of the employees of the office in
which he worked.

Starting with the office boy, he went through the entire list up
to and including the president of the company. This last lunch-

eon was the greatest experience of all. For the president with moist eyes said:

"I have been president of this company for twelve years and you are the first of the employees who has ever invited me to lunch. I was so thrilled that I cancelled a luncheon date with two prominent bankers to be your guest."

Three years of opening the church and one caller! But the far-reaching results of this one meeting more than justified the time spent. For my friend, suddenly realizing that he should know all his fellow employees, was inspired to greatly widen his circle of friendships.

Jesus went up on a mountain to make his decisions and receive inspiration. Through the ages spiritual power has been much more available under conditions of solitude and quiet. There is no reason why we shouldn't relax and let God talk to us. We have some very busy and able people keeping our church open, and I have never yet heard of anyone who followed the rules and received no benefit.

The truth is that for some as yet inexplicable reason, a vision comes to us when in quietness we go to God for advice and courage and comfort. Not only do we see clearly the right road to follow, but we become capable of better applying our own abilities. In fact, we make full use of our physical and mental powers only when we benefit from God's rays shining down upon us. Only under such conditions should we make important decisions.

And remember this motto. "After man's ways fail, try God's."

SINCE I LET GOD TAKE OVER

by

Harry G. Heckmann

*Failure never fazed Harry Heckmann. He made
an astonishing comeback and promptly gave the
credit to God. This is the inspiring story not only
of a successful business man but of an equally successful personality.*

I WAS BROUGHT UP IN A RELIGIOUS HOME. LATER I BECAME A
church member and for years was more or less active in religious
affairs. Yet, I never really understood how the power of God applies to my everyday affairs. Like thousands of others, I went my
own way and depended solely upon myself. I was reasonably successful, and many friends and associates looked upon me as one
who was making good in life. Yet I was never satisfied; I was inwardly worried and I longed for happiness and peace.

I had created and organized a $300,000-a-year manufacturing
business. In 1931, during the depression, this business failed, and
I had to make a new start in life.

Today I have a prosperous business and a well-equipped farm.
I am making what I believe is a success in life. I am happy, in
good health, free from debt, free from worry. I have a host of
friends, and I really enjoy life.

I began to think seriously about my personal life and affairs
about ten years ago. Believing that there must be a correct way
to live and enjoy life, I decided to take my problems to God. I

asked Him to show me how I could get the most out of my life.

A few days later I received in the mail a religious booklet (I never knew who sent it to me), which seemed to have the answer. It gave me an entirely new slant on life. I began to realize that actually I had never wholly believed in the power of God to help me in my daily problems, difficulties, and worries. I simply lacked sufficient confidence or faith in the thing I professed to believe in. So, with absolute confidence in the result, I decided to let God run my affairs.

After some experiences in which wisdom and sound judgment in making decisions were needed, I realized that I must have more poise and better self-control in the presence of other people. My solution was a resolve to look for the good in every person with whom I come in contact. Whenever I meet a person, I say to myself, "I see the good in you and I thank God for this." Also, in whatever work I have to do, I look for the good in that.

To look for the good in everyone I meet and to find good in everything I do required practice. I had to acquire new habits of thought. When I attained them, a great change had been made in my life. No longer do I experience petty annoyances when meeting people, and they appear to sense this. I have poise, self-control, and a feeling of relaxation which relieves me of all tenseness.

My business is to sell two manufacturers' products in Greater New York. In the morning I am usually the first to reach my office. I ask God to guide my efforts during the day, and I thank Him in advance for answer to my prayer.

Before starting out to interview prospective customers it is my practice to pray by name for each man. I do not pray that I may make a sale, for emphasis upon self interest would tend to break the circuit. It would be dictating to God who may not want a sale made on that particular visit, or on any other visit for that matter. I merely pray for my customer as a man, asking that God may bless him in all his problems.

The result is that we meet in an atmosphere of friendliness and confidence. I have often noted that we are strangely attuned. Naturally sales result often far beyond my expectations. New accounts come to me in amazing and unexpected ways. Moreover, I have been privileged to help people whom otherwise I would never have contacted. It lifts business above money-making to the plane of human understanding.

Even in these days, when the problem is not to stimulate sales but to get merchandise to sell, this formula of trust and guidance also works. I am able to keep calm and handle each problem as it arises, and in strange ways overcome difficulties which in former years would have floored me completely.

For example, several years ago I visited a western city to see the president of a large manufacturing corporation regarding a business transaction of thousands of dollars. Three weeks before he had flatly rejected a proposal I had outlined in a letter. I had utmost confidence that my plan was sound in principle; therefore, on the journey west I prayed with faith about it. I asked God to direct me, to put the mind and heart of this man in a receptive attitude to reconsider his decision; and I actually believed that He would do this for me.

Five minutes after I entered his office, the president of the company suddenly reversed himself and said: "All right, I'll go along with you on this, and I'll leave it up to you to carry out the details."

Fifteen minutes before my arrival he had advised the general manager that he was still opposed to my plan. Of course, the corporation's officers were simply amazed at this sudden change of mind. To them, it was a miracle. To me, it was a direct answer to my prayers.

This and many similar experiences have given me great faith in the practical results of prayer. They give me courage and self-confidence. Prayer relieves me of tension; it enables me to think clearly and to maintain a calm and confident attitude toward life.

Prayer has make me more tolerant of other folks. I have learned to expect and find the good in them. This has helped me to work more in harmony with my associates. I find that now they put more confidence in me.

As God reveals Himself and His power to me more and more every day, I truly believe that I have found the secret of life. He keeps me cheerful, happy, confident, forward-looking, and free from negative thoughts. Of course, one must play fair with God when asking favors of Him; and that I have tried to do. Through all this experience my devoted wife shared the same belief and faith, and this has been added inspiration.

The same opportunity is open to everyone who is willing to trust in God, and to put one's affairs entirely in His care. Are you willing to let God take over?

OUR ONE
AND ONLY PROBLEM

by

Stella Terrill Mann

One real problem—only one. Those who solve it find life smoothing out into a glorious adventure. Stella Terrill Mann, successful short story writer and author of the book Change Your Life Through Prayer, *presents the problem and suggests the answer.*

ONCE I THOUGHT THERE WERE AS MANY PROBLEMS IN LIFE AS there were hours in my day. Once I felt that life was hardly worth the living. That was before I learned the truth—that there is *but one problem in all the world,* and that it is our failure to solve this one problem which gives rise to all the other troublesome and heartbreaking situations of life.

There are not millions of problems facing our post-war world. There are not hundreds of problems facing every citizen of chaotic America to which the rest of the world now looks for help. There are not as many problems in your own individual life as you might unhappily believe. There is but *one* problem.

For a number of years it has been my privilege to work with people in trouble. These people were from all walks of life. They included rich and poor, ignorant and educated, men and women, young and old. Among them were professional people, housewives, laborers, business men and women, doctors, educators and others. There were Jews, Gentiles of no religion and Christians of both Protestant and Catholic faith. There were Americans, Englishmen, Negroes, Japanese and other members of the human family.

In the whole group, no two people were alike. Yet they had one thing in common. a load of trouble. In the final analysis we always found that they had but *one* problem and when they learned how to solve that, they solved everything else in their lives that had been worrying them. And I found further, that they all had the same and one and only problem.

What *is* this one problem?

It is not to learn how to pile up a great fortune for one's self and posterity. I have worked with people who have piled up fortunes and either lost them, or suffered the tortures of the damned by never having learned to solve that one problem I have worked with adults whose pitiful condition grew out of the misspent lives of their parents who had been cursed with too much money.

Yet money in itself is neither a curse nor a blessing. People who learned to solve that *one* problem have created fortunes, greatly blessed themselves and others, or having a fortune, found the solution to keeping it while sharing it and living a satisfying life. Every man and woman I have ever known who had created an honest and lasting fortune had learned to solve that one problem.

What *is* the one problem?

It is not how to build up physical health. Because many have perfect health, yet are so beset by unhappiness, complications of affairs, poverty, a hundred negative conditions that life is a drag instead of a glorious adventure.

I have worked with people who had both health and a fortune who, never having solved the *one* problem, were in turmoil, grief and living under threats they could no longer bear and were driven to seek help. Yet there are many who have frail health, some who are blind, deaf, others who have lost a body member or two, who still live radiant, useful and self-supporting lives because they have solved that *one* problem.

What *is this one* problem?

It is not how to find friends, to love and to be loved. It is not how to be popular and appreciated, to feel important in a world of people. No, for we see the greatly loved and highly popular and securely placed fall to the depths of despair, and even to suicide, because they were lonely and lost in spite of every outward appearance.

I worked with a woman who had everything that money and love of a husband, children, relatives and friends could give her, whose every problem was solved for her but the one problem. She became an alcoholic, sometimes staying drunk for weeks, because she could not face life. To me she wept, "I hate myself! Inside I am all hollow Nothing means anything!" She found the meaning of life, the worth of love, and that she was not "all hollow inside" when she learned how to solve that one problem.

What *is this one problem?*

It is not how to go search the ends of the earth for wisdom, not to learn how to follow great thinkers, read the works of the learned of earth since time began. No. For the meek and lowly, the uneducated and the "unwashed," the poor, often furnish us with absolute proof that to solve the one and only problem, is to solve the meaning of life and how to live.

What then, is this one problem?

It is so simple you will hardly believe me. But if you and enough others will join you in so solving it, we shall have heaven on earth. Now listen: Our only problem as an individual, a Nation, a World, is to *learn how to communicate* with the great Infinite Spirit, Creator of the Universe, Creator of Man, Father of all, which we commonly call God. This procedure we commonly call prayer. The whole trouble lies in the fact that so few know what prayer really is, and fewer still know how to use it effectively. That is why I use the term communicate, for it expresses my exact meaning. Communicate means what Webster says, "To have intercourse; be connected." And to further define the meaning, Webster says intercourse means, "interchange of thought and feeling."

To restate my assertion· There is but one problem in all the world, and that is, to learn how to connect with God, and to experience an interchange of thought and feeling with Him.

Tremendous Truth! Life giving Truth for the individual! World saving Truth for the human family! Not begging God, not telling God what to do, but communicating with Him. We must learn to find God, to speak, to listen, for having heard we wish to obey. For we learn what life is, and how to live. Having learned we desire above all else that kind of life, for in it we find the outer world becoming like our honest heart's desire and inner hopes, just as Jesus promised we should.

We do not need more great scientists and inventors to give us new technological marvels, new ways of counter-offensives in war. No. What we are dying for lack of, is more people in high and low places the world over to learn the marvel of finding God and of communicating with Him. That is the only way we shall ever end war. And every great living scientist knows it!

Every responsible business man surely realizes that the greatest need in our economic life today is not how to make more gadgets to save more time, to earn more money. No, far from it. What the economic world needs and industry is killing itself off for lack of, is for human beings to learn how to get along together as brothers! This means management, labor and capital. And representatives of each have admitted as much to me.

Our tax burdens threaten modern civilization. Crime is one of the heaviest loads the tax payer carries. Crime is on the increase. Yet every criminal could be healed of his criminal tendencies by being taught the reality of Life. No man having found God, having actually communicated with Him, could ever enter a life of crime. We have failed to teach our young people how to find God. Our failure here has given rise to crime, excessive drinking and child delinquency.

One problem—only one. Those who solve it find life smoothing out into a glorious adventure. Such a one finds there are no problems, only steps that lead ever out and ever up, with no problems, but challenges, attempts, success, and thrilling rewards

And how does one go about learning how to solve this **one** problem? Your Bible, your minister, or any one of many **good** books on the subject, or your friends who have solved it, can **give** you the answer.

If you earnestly seek, you will find the answer. Believe **me.** *I know.*

SO WHAT!

Grove Patterson

"Sometimes a slang expression can actually solve problems" So says Grove Patterson, editor of the Toledo Blade *and one of the most dynamic speakers and personalities in this country.*

I HAVE NEVER CARED DEEPLY FOR SLANG, FEELING THAT A FRE-
quent resort to it indicates a lack of appreciation of the limitless
resources of the world's richest language. For English is the most
amazing tool ever devised by mankind for the communication of
ideas. Of course, slang is a part of the language and some of it is
both vividly expressive and highly convincing. It is chiefly the
resort of the mentally lazy.

But there is one slang expression, of fairly recent coinage,
which has profound meaning and, I think, real value. I refer to
the phrase, "So what?"

Now there is a philosophic expression which can actually solve
problems! I have an idea that we can apply it to about fifty per
cent of our troubles, our frets and worries and griefs, and find that
it is a comfortable cure-all. I know a so-called big industrialist
who is forever worrying about trivialities. He is constantly engaged in post mortems. No matter how trivial the error, he persists
in re-examining it from all angles. The right answer, which he
doesn't know, to practically all his fulminations is, "So what?"
When he has reached the stage of tranquillity that will enable him
thus to reply to his own analysis, he will be a much happier
person.

I am a frequent victim of my own post mortems. I sometimes lie awake nights trying to figure out why I did this or that, or didn't do it, and all the time the easy conclusion is within my grasp: "So what?"

Many of us complain because of our lot in life when it is completely evident there is nothing we can do about it. "So what?" We didn't ask to be born, but here we are! "So what?" Others complain about circumstances which they could change if they had the courage and the energy. Such as they do not deserve a philosophy. Such as they do not deserve this wholly satisfying phrase. I speak mostly of and for those who seek to re-pour the water that has gone under the bridge.

When we finally come to learn that many things come to all of us which we cannot do anything about, we shall have put a broad and sturdy plank into the foundation of our philosophy.

I should like to say further that this satisfying conclusion, "So what?", is not solely adaptable to the lighter, more trivial experiences of life. It is there to comfort men and women in the midst of profound sorrow. When we have lost much that we have worked for in life, lost the companionship of ones we love, we may not resort to a slang phrase but we certainly can, and indeed might just as well, resort to the simple philosophy of which it is expressive. Do we suffer? Yes of course, for that is the way of all flesh. Is there anything we can do about it, other than to confront the circumstances with whatever dignity and nobility that lie within us? We shall then do as well as we can. "So what?"

My religious convictions, my faith that life has meaning and purpose and direction, have enabled me to arrive at this simple philosophy. St. Paul talks sense when he says: "Having done all, stand."

Do the best you know. Do the best you are able to do. That is all you or any man can do. I still believe that "duties are ours; results are God's." Let us stand—and forget it.

Home—Center of Happiness

RELIGION GUIDED
MY CAREER

by

Cecil B. deMille

One of Hollywood's greatest pioneers and most famous figures found strength and guidance through his boyhood religious training. As a result Cecil B. deMille was inspired to produce such notable motion pictures as Ten Commandments, King of Kings, *and* The Sign of the Cross. *Mr. deMille is president of Cecil B. deMille Productions, Inc., and has organized, and is president of the Mercury Aviation Company in Hollywood, California.*

YEARS AGO IN NEW YORK CITY AN INTERVIEWER APPROACHED me. "Mr. deMille," he said, "I want to ask you a rather personal question—a question which few interviewers may have asked you —but one to which many people would like an answer. *I want to know what the finest religious memory of your life has been.*"

That one hit me squarely between the eyes. Religion has always been a vital part of both my home life and my career, but I was hesitant to discuss it openly. Still it was a good question, put differently by Thomas Carlyle. "The chief thing about a man is his religion."

I recalled my boyhood days when my father's vivid reading of the Bible had so profoundly influenced me. Then a particularly significant incident came into my mind . . . the occasion when a minister performed a complete church service with but a solitary boy in the congregation.

I never will forget this minister, with prominent red beard, who once came to preach for a week in my home town of Pompton, New Jersey. I was ten at the time. My father was one of the supports of our community church and acted as lay reader when the church could not afford a resident minister.

The visiting minister announced he would preach each day during Passion Week at an early morning service—eight o'clock as I recall. The morning I planned to attend dawned cold and rainy. I walked alone to the church through a murky morning gloom When I arrived I observed no one was present but myself and the red-bearded minister. I was the congregation.

Embarrassed, I took a seat, wondering anxiously what he would do. The hour for the service arrived. With calm and solemn dignity the minister walked into the pulpit. Then he looked down on me and smiled—a smile of great dignity and sincerity. In the congregation sat a solitary child, but he commenced the service as if the church was crowded to the walls.

A ritual opened the services, followed by a reading lesson to which I gave the responses. Then the minister preached a short sermon. He talked earnestly to me—and to God. When it came time for the offering, he stepped down from the pulpit and put the collection plate on the altar railing. I walked up and dropped my nickel into the plate.

Then he did a beautiful thing. He left the pulpit and came down to the altar to receive my offering. As he did this he placed his hand on my head. I can feel the thrill and sensation of that gentle touch to this day.

In walking back to my seat that day I knew this man's God was a real God, and that his faith was God-like in its monumental simplicity. It left a lump in my throat, and I cannot think of it even today without emotion. That was religion at its finest. It won my belief and strengthened my faith. I knew that the spirit of truth had been in that church with us.

This incident has had more recent significance. Many of us reach middle age and beyond, with the fear that our lives have been useless, wasted. Is it not possible that we—parents, preachers, teachers, writers, actors, editors, etc.—might have deeply influenced a child or grown-up as did the red-bearded minister? Many of us have changed human lives for the better without knowing it. In moments of unhappiness and discouragement this thought helps sustain me.

When asked what it was that turned my mind toward the making of great Biblical motion pictures, I again trace back through the years to find the influence that first awakened my mind to the spiritual power of Biblical scenes. I have always been aware that the Bible was a "best seller," that more human beings have been interested in Bible stories than in any other stories on earth.

As a boy, however, I used to sit on the arm of a big leather chair every evening as my father read two chapters of the Bible, one from the Old Testament and one from the New. It was a family custom. My father, having been a writer of note in his day, read anything well, but he especially liked to read the Bible. He made the words come alive; the characters moved and breathed before our eyes. It seemed to us he touched the beauty and drama in every story, and our eyes glistened with excitement, then were wet with tears.

My father's great vulnerable point was that he loved to have his head rubbed. We children knew of this weakness and used it to our advantage. So absorbed did we become in the Bible stories that we hated to have him stop. So, I used to sit on the arm of his old leather chair, by pre-arrangement with the other children in the family, and rub his head as he read. So soothed and relaxed did he become that he would forget the hour and go on reading extra chapters to us as we sat intently around his chair.

I have no doubt that my father's vivid reading of Biblical stories planted in my impressionable mind a reverence and respect for the Bible, perhaps even a sense of its dramatic values, which in subsequent years was to turn me to the Great Book for themes to thrill motion picture audiences.

It was always a battle to get support and backing for Biblical pictures. Producers feared them on the basis such pictures would not yield enough to pay the enormous expenses involved. That was true with *The Ten Commandments, The King of Kings, The Sign of the Cross,* and *The Crusades.* However, they more than paid their way in both financial and spiritual benefits, and some are still playing in various parts of the world.

Years ago I heard of an interesting incident that occurred when *The King of Kings* was exhibited in Constantinople A crowd of hoodlums came to the theatre to break up the show, and began by hooting and throwing things. In a few minutes the rowdyism stopped. The hoodlums were subdued by the beauty and sacredness of the theme. At the end they sheepishly admitted to the manager that they had come to scoff and—almost—remained to pray. A story of the incident was contained in an Associated Press dispatch.

I have been in Hollywood since 1913, during which time actors, actresses, directors and producers have passed in seemingly endless procession, some befriended by destiny, other lost in oblivion. In a maelstrom like Hollywood there are many reasons for failure and unhappiness. I believe the chief among these is the failure to realize that *the purpose of this life is understanding of the spirit and not worship before the calf of gold.*

PARENTS
ARE NOT ENOUGH

by

J. Edgar Hoover

The man who trapped the notorious killer, Dillinger—the most effective hunter of criminals in America, J Edgar Hoover—puts the finger on the crime of parents against the welfare of their children. A great advocate of Christianity, Mr. Hoover has been Director since 1924 of the Federal Bureau of Investigation, U. S. Department of Justice.

I HAVE CLOSELY FOLLOWED CRIMINAL ACTIVITY IN THE UNITED States, particularly during the last twenty-three years. I have seen its results I have come face to face with those who laugh at the law, who steal, rob, pillage and kill. I have fought against them in their attempts to slash away at our national character. At times it has been most discouraging to note the apathy and indifference of many of our citizens toward the steady rises in crime.

All during the war years major crime was on the upswing. It reached a sixteen-year peak in 1946. The fact that every 5.7 minutes of the day and night brings a crime of murder, manslaughter, rape or assault to kill is a challenge that should be answered by concerted action.

At the end of the recent war, age seventeen led all other age groups in arrest for serious crimes. We now have a state of affairs where the juvenile offender has grown up and graduated into serious crimes of murder, robbery and assault. A general moral decadence in the United States is emphasized by the arrest in 1946 of 108,787 young people under twenty-one years of age for crimes serious enough to warrant finger-printing.

How shall we explain this situation?

What constructive action can we take to alleviate the problem?

The answer lies for the most part in the homes of the nation. Many of the cases coming to my attention reveal the shocking fact that *parents are forgetting their God-given and patriotic obligations to the little ones.* In a spirit of recklessness and abandonment they are neglecting the children entrusted to their care. How can we blame youngsters who are ashamed of their mothers and feel that their fathers do not represent honorable manhood? The conduct of many parents today is directly attributable to the breakdown in youthful morals and character.

I recall one case where four boys, aged sixteen and seventeen, banded together and perpetrated a series of housebreakings and thefts. Three of the boys were victims of broken homes. Parental control was lacking in the life of the fourth boy. The mother of one of the youngsters had been carrying on an illicit affair with a man in the absence of her husband. Her son knew this and definitely resented the immorality of his mother. He lost the incentive to maintain good conduct and a good reputation for himself.

In another case, a boy first came to the attention of the police when he was ten years of age. He had the questionable distinction of first testing his skill in thievery in his own home at the expense of his father. The boy's subsequent activities ranged from housebreaking to armed robbery. The youngster's parents unwittingly contributed to his delinquency by placing their employment and other interests foremost. As a result the boy was neglected.

The pattern of these cases is repeated over and over again. More and more children are being sacrificed upon the altar of indifference as parents throw aside responsibility. Selfishness is the keynote of the day and materialism the inspiration for living.

God in many instances is not accepted in the home and concepts of morality have been relegated to the junk heap.

Can a nation exist void of all religious thought and action? Can we have internal peace without morality? Can we build homes without God or have worthy parents who know not His teachings? Who is the fountainhead of justice, equity, truth, goodness and majestic integrity? What is the reason for life, its aims and its end?

The key to these problems, to life itself, is God. He is man's first need—his final goal. Religion, the bond that binds man to God, is the golden arch that leads to happiness. Destroy it and chaos will result.

The home built upon firm Christian principles is a fortress against evil. Those who live within are crusaders for decency—disciples of democracy. A Godless home is built upon sand. Buffeted by the tides of envy, avarice, greed and sloth, the structure weakens and finally crumbles. Decay seeps into the physical and moral structure and crime finds an inviting breeding ground.

My hope for the future of this nation is predicated upon the faith in God which is nurtured in the home. No outside influence of a constructive nature can overcome the lack of a guiding light in the home. If the trend toward crime is to be met, the spark of this light must be the knowledge of God and its fuel must be the understanding of Him and His works

Parents must awaken to the realization that the family is the first great training school in behavior or misbehavior. Children develop a sense of right and wrong—they are not born with it. The home becomes for them their first classroom and parents serve as their first teachers for the inspirational education of youth.

Through the medium of the home, the child must learn to appreciate the necessity for discipline and the need for law and order to guide the conduct of people in society. He must absorb lessons of good citizenship and recognize that he has the responsibility to take his place as a citizen in the United States.

Above all, he must be taught a love and a knowledge of God. If these qualities are exemplified and taught in the family circle, the child will be fortified with a character that will be a forceful antidote against temptation.

No home can be sound unless it is built on a strong foundation of moral fortitude. The lack of proper moral training may hush the conscience to such a degree that man's ultimate end will be misery. There can be no strong moral fibre in the nation unless man binds himself to God He does this through religion.

Our nation is sadly in need of a rebirth of the simple life—a return to the days when God was a part of each household, when families arose in the morning with a prayer on their lips and ended the day by placing themselves in His care. We should revive the beautiful practice of offering thanksgiving at meals and bring back to the family circle the moments when father or mother unfolded the beautiful lessons of the Bible to eager, young listeners

The foundation of our democracy was built upon a firm faith in the Almighty. As our nation grew and prospered, as it overcame vicissitudes and adversities, its people never lost faith in a personal God Our generation, it seems, has allowed old, faithful religious practices to slip into oblivion As a result, the nation has suffered and its children have become spiritually starved.

Let us return to the faith of our fathers and reap once again the harvest of God's blessings.

SO LONG
UNTIL TOMORROW

by

Lowell Thomas

*The voice of Lowell Thomas, famed radio com-
mentator, is a familiar one everywhere. List the
world's great adventurers from Marco Polo to the
present, and Lowell Thomas stands high in that
glorious company.*

FOR MOST OF MY LIFE, IT SEEMS, I HAVE BEEN SAYING TO SOME-
body, "So long until tomorrow." The opportunity for a life not
entirely lacking in adventure has been mine—poking around in
some of the far-away corners of the world.

Every man, I suppose, can single out the people and the places
that have had the greatest influence on his life. And surely one of
the prime factors in heading me for wherever I've gone was the
fact that during my boyhood years we lived on a mountaintop in
the Rockies, at ten thousand feet, where we could see in three
directions for about a hundred and fifty miles. Spread out to the
west, south and north of us was one of the most awe-inspiring
sights in all this world—the Sangre de Cristo range (the "Blood of
Christ" range).

And what made that scene all the more sublime was that it was
never the same. The kaleidoscopic colors, the drifting clouds, the
vast, mysterious distances, always changing. Against the horizon,
in a far-sweeping arc, their snowy fourteen-thousand-foot peaks
tinted pink by the Alpine glow, stood more lofty mountains than

the eye of mere man is likely to behold at one time, anywhere else on this planet. How could it fail to move one deeply, to put its mark on a youngster who stood on those heights marveling at the panorama, day after day, month after month, year after year?

The immensity of it left its mark on me in many ways. In its impact upon mind and soul it was like living on the rim of the Grand Canyon. Nothing I have ever known has equalled it.

Living on that mountaintop during the formative years of my life played a part in charting the course of all the years that have followed. From our mountain the world seemed to stretch out before me. I could hear voices calling from the other side of the Sangre de Cristo, urging me to follow trails of adventure to the far places of the world, along the Golden Road to Samarkand.

But, my father gave me other and still greater vistas. My father had been a student of almost every subject under the sun. In some respects I think he is the most highly educated man I have ever known. Religion, philosophy, geology, zoology, botany, literature, astronomy—he studied them all. And his curiosity and enthusiasm for all things he passed on to me. He would get me up at all hours of the night, even when it was below zero, to show me things that could not be seen earlier in the night: astronomical phenomena of startling beauty in the rarefied night sky of our ten-thousand-foot eyrie.

He would point out some celestial marvel against the backdrop of the mighty mountains and, being a deeply spiritual man, he tied all of that up with God. (At two or three A.M. my own boyhood reaction was not quite so spiritual!) Nevertheless, he gave me a conception of the spiritual quality of the universe that has gone with me as I have roamed the earth.

The wide range of my father's reading couldn't help but affect me. He was always a liberal in his thoughts, and was constantly seeking for new light and deeper truth. From him I acquired a tremendous concept of a tremendous God. He gave me both patience and impatience with pettiness in religion.

My friends have often remarked that I seem too interested and

SO LONG UNTIL TOMORROW [223]

enthusiastic about everything. If so, then my father is to blame. He used to take me on trips, jaunts on which we talked about the origin of the earth. He had a scientific point of view, and never entertained mechanical notions about the beginning of the universe. To him it was entirely spiritual He saw the Hand of God in everything.

Many times in our home he would spend long periods reading to me from what he believed to be the greatest Book in the world, the Bible. He did not read the Bible to us in the usual stereotyped form of family prayers, but as a scholar would read from any great work. He read it to me because the Book was bubbling out of him; it was part of his life.

He put these Biblical stories into my bloodstream And, suddenly, they all became a part of the background of the climactic experience of my life, the period when I was with Allenby's army and with the Arabs under Lawrence in "The Revolt in the Desert." These armies were fighting across lands where the Israelites wandered, and although I had never seen these regions until I joined Allenby, it all seemed like familiar territory because I had been over it in imagination many times with my father.

This was by far the peak of my life For a thousand years it had been the dream of Western peoples and of Christian Civilization to free the Holy Land from the Infidel. And the Turks of Abdul Hamid's day and the armies of Envor Pasha were the direct successors to the Saracens of old. When Allenby freed Palestine, with the aid of Lawrence and his Bedouin raiders, that, to me, was the last and the greatest of the Crusades to capture the Holy Sepulchre

Eagerly I explored the places of historic interest. Gaza, home of Delilah, where Samson pulled down the mighty pillars of the temple. Through the land of Abraham and of Lot, from Beersheba to Dan, I wandered. And every step of the way had its thrills.

On the Plain of Ezdraclon I camped. And we journeyed up and down the road to Jerusalem time and time again. It all seemed familiar, as though I had walked it before. As indeed I had, in thought, at our home on that ten-thousand-foot peak, near Cripple Creek, in Colorado. There a devout and scholarly father had read those Bible stories until these lands seemed to belong to me. As I rode with Allenby's cavalry, the Bible came to life, and I seemed to be a part of the great stream of history, a participant in dramatic events.

My first view of Jerusalem from a two-seater plane was one of the breath-taking experiences of my life. At last I was looking down on the Holy City of Christendom, "aloof, waterless, and on the road to nowhere." To look down on Jerusalem from the sky in the early morning, to get your first glimpse of this, the holiest city in the world—there can be few greater thrills than that.

I have referred to the philosophical and religious background of my father. My mother gave me a touch of the old-time religion. And the two are a good mixture.

The Church has always been a vital part of my life. To me it is part of life just the same as the public schools, the same as the government in Washington, the same as our meals during the day. Just a normal part of the process of living. One of those things you don't often think about, to question or analyze—any more than you analyze your wife. She is part of everything. So also is the Church a part of everything. I have never given much thought to the Church from the standpoint of analyzing it or speculating about it. It is just a normal, natural part of a daily experience I am tremendously enthusiastic about recommending that people attend church.

One of the great guideposts of my life was given me by my father who said, in effect: "You live in a great world; keep moving always toward greater things. Keep mountaintop experiences alive in your mind." Guideposts, to me, point to something ever beyond, not yet reached. . . . So long, until tomorrow.

IS GRATITUDE
A "ONE DAY SPECIAL"?

by

Ted Malone

A warm, homey picture of a family scene told by Ted Malone, radio personality, war correspondent and book and poetry anthologist. Widely known for his inspiring feature "Between the Bookends," Ted Malone is heard over a coast-to-coast network five days a week.

IT HAPPENED LAST THANKSGIVING. MY DAUGHTER HAPPY—SHE was seven then—dashed in the house, threw herself breathlessly into the big green chair by the bookcase and asked, "Daddy, why is Thanksgiving?"

"Why is Thanksgiving?" . . . The old trite answer came first: "Well, it's a day set aside to give thanks."

"Tell me, Daddy, what have you given thanks about?"

What had I given thanks about? I remember one gloomy, rainy night in London. I had gone to Waterloo Station to watch the evacuation of the children. The big dim-lighted station was an eerie place that night. I had watched troops come and depart there many times . . . but this was different . . . little children! Where were they all going? Would they be safe there? Would the brothers and sisters, most of whom were clutching one another's hands now, be able to stay together? Certainly not all would.

I told Happy about that night, and explained that had she

been there, had we been an English family, she would probably have been one of those children going away.

"I'd have taken Mommie with me."

"You couldn't have. That's why I happened to think about that night. All children five and over had to go alone, like parcels with labels around their necks. You see, back in the United States you were having your birthday party. You were five years old."

"Then that was my birthday, July 21! That wasn't Thanksgiving."

I admitted it. "But I was never more thankful for anything than that you were not in London that night."

"What else have you had Thanksgiving about, Daddy?"

"What else?" Tell it again. Favorite phrases of childhood. Once more I searched my memory. "There was the time, several years ago, that my contract with a radio network had come to an end and had not been renewed I was out of a job for the first time since college days. What if I couldn't get another one? Unemployed! The word scared me. Then your Mommie calmly said something I'll never forget. 'Unemployed? Why you're just having a holiday. You've worked hard for ten years. You deserve a holiday' My fear, my humiliation, my worry vanished. I took a holiday and I found another job."

"On Thanksgiving, Daddy?"

"No—I didn't find the job on Thanksgiving."

"Oh, Mommie told you on Thanksgiving."

"No. Come to think about it, that 'Thanksgiving Day' happened in April. That day your mother's faith in me gave me new faith in myself, and that's a good thing to have on Thanksgiving or any day in the year."

To my surprise Happy said matter-of-factly, "I know about faith. Grandfather told me "

"Your grandfather taught me about faith too," I said.

"On Thanksgiving?"

I started to say no, and then changed it to: "On all the days of his life."

Happy looked up expectantly and then settled back, as I began: "In the summer of 1873 there was a little boy born on a farm near Bennet, Iowa. Even as a boy he didn't like to farm, but he helped his brothers and sisters to do the farm chores. He went to husking bees and box suppers and played 'Hi Jim Along Josey' at the country parties.

"He fairly rushed through his youth eating bowls of bread and milk for supper every night, planting and husking corn, trying to decide what he was going to be when he grew up. In America a boy can dream and try anything he has the courage to attempt.

"So one summer he decided to be a salesman, a traveling salesman. He set out to sell folding blackboards. His first day, partly as a joke, he took a big black cigar because someone told him salesmen always smoked cigars. And he smoked it. But it wasn't a joke. It made him deathly sick. That was the first and last time he ever smoked. His summer business was almost as disastrous. He ended up in debt. But he didn't get mad; he didn't decide the world was unfair to him. He just chalked up the summer as an interesting adventure and went back to school to find a way to make himself more valuable.

"Some folks think you have to be rich or famous to be happy, but this boy decided that you get more happiness out of the things you do for the world than what you depend on it to do for you. So he set out to increase the happiness of others. He became a minister and started to preach the gospel.

"He travelled from town to town. Sometimes he preached in a tent, and sometimes in a school house. Sometimes when evening came he would put his torchlight up on his wagon, then set up a small pump organ and sing until the crowd gathered."

"What happened when it rained?"

"Well I'll tell you, Happy. He did then just as he'd always done —made the best of things. I remember he told me that whenever I was worried about any kind of storm to remember a Psalm they often read at these meetings. It begins: 'The Lord is my shepherd; I shall not want.'"

Happy supplied the second line: " 'He maketh me to lie down in green pastures: he leadeth me beside the still waters.' I know that one—I've heard it on the radio."

"I expect you have. It's my favorite."

"Where did grandfather stay all night?"

"He stayed wherever he was invited. Sometimes the places were clean and comfortable. Sometimes dirty, and he would have to sleep on the floor."

Happy interrupted me. "That mustn't have been much fun."

"Well, I never heard him complain. You see, in between the storms he was always finding people who were discouraged and bitter, people who were searching for something they could believe in. . . . And giving people faith, people who need it, well, that is fun.

"Later in life your Grandfather ran a grocery store, and then he became a candy manufacturer. But whatever business he was in, he ran it just as he had run his life . . . with complete faith in his fellowmen.

"This summer on his seventy-fourth birthday, we all joined in 'Thanksgiving' that his heart is still full of the songs he has sung since college days; that his years are rich with a host of friends. Just by his simple goodness he has taught the happiness than can come through faith."

"This summer!" Happy bounced out of the chair. "Looks like Thanksgiving never really comes in November."

"Of course it does," I told her. "And these stories show that it comes on other days, too. When the last Thursday in November comes, the real Thanksgiving Day, we can just add up all the year's happiness. Everybody can be happy then."

Happy thought a minute. "Everybody but one—the turkey!"

HE LET THE FACE OF GOD SHINE THROUGH

by

William L. Stidger

Walt Whitman, Buffalo Bill, Theodore Roose-
velt and Will Rogers all rolled into one is the way
Dr. William L. Stidger has been characterized. It
isn't often that a theological professor is thus de-
scribed, but Dr. Stidger has the human touch.

I FOUND GOD THROUGH MY FATHER.

As Edna St. Vincent Millay says in a couplet:

> *"The soul can split the skies in two*
> *And let the face of God shine through."*

My father was a perfect illustration of that couplet. Jesus said, "He that hath seen me hath seen the Heavenly Father."

The first memory I have of my saintly father was on an unforgetable spring Sunday when he took me by the hand and walked me up to the top of a West Virginia hill. It was a stiff hard climb, and my legs ached before we got to the top. Toward the end of the climb my father, who was walking out ahead, kept yelling back at me: "Come a little higher, son! Come a little higher!"

Finally, I caught up with him, and we stopped and turned. Miles and miles of dazzling terrain stretched out before our eyes. My father pointed out the winding curve of the beautiful Ohio River, the hills of Ohio beyond the river.

"The higher you climb, the more beautiful it becomes," he said. "The farther up you get, the wider your vision and the more you can see. It's a great and glorious world, son."

Just then a red cardinal flashed past us and alighted on a mountain laurel twig. The laurel was a pinkish white and the leaves a deep green. That crimson cardinal was such a flash of color against that green background that I have never forgotten it.

"That's a cardinal bird, son. We call it a red bird, but bird experts call it a cardinal. God made the cardinals, the Baltimore orioles, the red-winged blackbirds, the scarlet tanagers, the eagle and the wrens. God did a beautiful thing when He made the birds, didn't He?"

And somehow on that immortal morning, my father introduced me to God in a simple, convincing fashion, which made Him seem very real to me.

On another memorable Sunday afternoon my father and I were sitting on our front porch when Max Bachenheimer, our town's only Jew, walked by. He smiled as father greeted him. Then my father told me what a fine, generous family man Max was. He told me how hard Max worked and what a good citizen he was; how faithful he was to his duties. That same afternoon one of our town Negroes also passed by. He was a simple, faithful soul, worked hard, took good care of his large family, always attended church and tithed his small income. All of this my father told me simply and naturally, and I drank it in.

Then my father said to me: "Max is a good father, son. He loves his family and looks after them like a father should. That is the way God does. He is the Father of the whole human family, and we are all a part of that family. That's why we pray 'Our Father' in 'The Lord's Prayer'." Through that simple explanation I came to look upon men of all colors, creeds and nations as a part of the Human Family. It is a simple formula—but it works.

My father had another simple way of teaching us to see God. He conducted family worship each morning. All five of us children knelt down on our knees at the breakfast table and father prayed for each one of us by name, starting with the youngest and going to the oldest.

"God bless, be with and care for, May, Reed, Anna, Nona and Willie." Then each of us went out into the day's activities, adventures and childhood problems with the memory of father taking each of our names to God.

A dramatic, tender and unforgettable experience which illustrates my father's devotion to the religious life of his children is the one I like to think of as "The Night of the Little Stockings." It happened this way:

Since my mother died when she was in her early thirties, my father had always felt a very deep and definite sense of responsibility for our religious development. There was no sacrifice that he would not make to see that the five of us got to Sunday school and church each Sunday. We always sat in the same church pew, and my father always sat there with us. He did not send us; he took us.

Since my father kept a little confectionery store, he had to work until around midnight on Saturdays. We children always went to sleep around nine o'clock and never knew when he got home from the store. But one Saturday night I found out, for I was restless. Shortly after midnight I was awakened by something dropping on the floor.

I looked up out of sleepy eyes, and my father, noticing that I was awake, said to me: "Sorry I awakened you, Willie. I dropped my darning egg."

Then he got down on his weary knees (he had worked from six that morning to midnight) and crawled halfway under my bed to retrieve his ivory darning egg. Watching him from sleep filled eyes, I saw him take that round smooth darning egg, settle himself into the rocking chair, insert the egg in the heel of a little stocking, stretch the wool heel of that stocking and clumsily, laboriously, but fairly accurately, darn the last little hole in it.

I dropped off to sleep again, but sometime later I was awakened by the light shining in my eyes. I yawned, stretched my arms, rubbed my eyes, then looked across the room. There sat my father sound asleep, with the darning egg dangling from his hand, his head slumped on his chest, but his task completed. Five pairs of little stockings lay in a neat row on the dresser.

I climbed out of bed, walked over to him, and shook him gently by the shoulder. "Father, you'd better get into bed to sleep."

He opened his eyes, then smiled a rueful smile. "Thank you, son. I was pretty tired tonight." He took me in his arms and kissed me. "Back to bed, Willie—and—God keep you!"

"God keep you!" was a favorite phrase of his. He never said, "God bless you" but always "God keep you."

But there was another experience, more intimate, personal and close than all of these. In my youth we had an old-fashioned revival in our Simpson Church. I, as an adolescent boy, fell under what was then called "Conviction." One evening I accepted the "Invitation" to go to the altar. They were singing "Just as I am without one plea but that Thy blood was shed for me." When they came to the phrase "Oh, Lamb of God, I come! I come!" I was so much in earnest, so eager that I almost ran down the center aisle of that church, threw myself on the altar, began to weep, pray and reach my soul out to—SOMETHING.

Then that SOMETHING came to me. It was simple, direct and certain . . . a great sense of peace, quiet, calm and assurance that I was at one with God. It was an ecstatic experience and yet a quiet one. I wanted to shout. I wanted to laugh and weep, and tell somebody. I opened my eyes, looked up—and right in front of me, kneeling on the other side of the sacred altar, was MY FATHER. He had seen me hurry down the aisle. He had followed me. He had gone on the inside of that altar to be near me, to pray with and for me. That was like my father. I found God that day never to lose Him; and my father was there when I found Him.

My father taught me to see God through Nature, through a social conception of the Great Human Family whose father was God, through family prayer and through a direct and simple religious experience.

"The soul can split the sky in two
And let the face of God shine through."

That was my father's way of leading me to see the face of God and it is still a good and a certain and a glorious way.

Improving Your Community Life

LET'S ROUT THE DEVIL WITH LOVE

by

Dorothy Canfield

"Variety is not only the spice of life . . . it is the necessity of life," Dorothy Canfield says. One of this country's most beloved writers gives a fresh approach to the problem of understanding among all races and creeds.

AN OLD COUSIN OF MINE DETESTED ONIONS. THAT WAS HIS RIGHT. But he also could not bear to have others say they liked onions. My old cousin at once was set off into an explosive attack on onions in an attempt to make them seem horrible in taste and smell.

You recognize him. Maybe you have had one like that in your family. You know how tiresome he is, and how narrow. He has forgotten that others think onions a great treat. Or that others enjoy them for variety. He has forgotten we need variety in our diet.

Suppose my old cousin were a powerful dictator and carried his narrowness far beyond mere tiresomeness into murderous insanity. Suppose, like the German Nazis, he decided to eliminate onions—froth at the mouth and shoot at people who ate them, or even used to grow them. Suppose he decided that oak trees were the only vegetation fit to live, and ordered people to rush out with axes, torches, poison, knives, and ploughs, to annihilate the abundant luxuriance of the countryside, leaving it one uniform

[237]

oak-forest. Oaks are all right. In fact, they are splendid. But what a calamity if there should be nothing but oaks. No nasturtiums, nor pumpkin vines, nor poplar-trees!

We surely must have learned by now, at least, that variety is not only the spice of life—it is the necessity of life.

One of the greatest human needs is the need for stability, expressed in the longing for a home of our own. Yet the need for travel and change is just as acute. We get warped, psychologically, if we don't have the shelter of a permanent home; but we get warped, psychologically, if we are always in it.

We need to do useful work. This, too, is a psychological need that is inescapable—as vital as the need for food to put into our mouths. People who do not do any useful work, but fool around with amusements or with occupations that are meaningless, or that are, worse still, spiritually destructive—these people become unbalanced, neurotic, victims of nervous ailments, and are always being sent to expensive sanitaria. But we all need a rest from useful work. Those who work incessantly without lifting their eyes and hearts to the fun, the beauty, the sheer thrill of life in general all about them, they also get neurotic and unbalanced and have to be sent to a retreat, or nursing home—some form of insane asylum!

We recognize this principle of variety in every activity of our whole lives. A mother must be wholly devoted to her children or they will not grow up well and strong. But she must not be *wholly* devoted to her children, or her affection will suffocate and smother them. We human beings not only like to have things both ways—like to have our cake and eat it too—but we *must*, by law of balance, combine two opposites in our lives or we can't be fulfilled and happy.

In no field have we, I think, so absurdly lost track of this fundamental law of variety as in the matter of those of our fellow men and women who are different from us. In general, our first instinct is not to like anyone different—in creed or race or skin-color. That is an imperious instinct. America alone—the melting pot—

has proven that all kinds can live together in harmony. But we have rather taken too much for granted this vitalizing American principle of the golden value of diversity in the population of a nation. It is really only since we have seen with shocked amazement the Nazi mania for cutting out of a nation all but one kind of person that we have begun to wake again to the true value of the American charm of diversity harmoniously adjusted.

It seems to me that we still talk too much about "tolerating" people different from us—instead of talking of our enthusiastic appreciation of the value of the multifarious differences which give this country its real interest, its real value, its moral beauty.

To love, whole heartedly, what you are protecting is as important, and far more life-giving, than to hate what you are attacking To make every positive effort to spread publicly our love for the splendid complexity of our human inheritance—that is as important as to hunt down and stamp out the manifestations of racial discrimination. Christ told us to *overcome evil with good.* Not to hate and attack evil.

To fight against something ugly, to keep down something hateful, is a call to perform with hate and anger, when really we are called upon to help, with joy, something beautiful to live; to protect, with love, something lovely and lovable—namely, the infinite variety in human beings which the Creator put on earth.

It's all right to attack intolerance as one attacks any kind of dirt. But to sing, instead, the praises of shining sunshiney cleanliness is far more heart-stirring and overcomes evil with good. To glorify the rich warm beauty of human diversity, to laugh heartily at the absurdity of the attempt to create dull monotony out of material so fascinatingly shimmering as the variety of human life. That calls for POSITIVE strength, not negative disapproval That is constructive—healing—and holy.

We are "the land of the free." Free for what? Free to develop, each of us, the best qualities he himself has, rather than to try to have the same qualities as those of everybody else. The essence of Americanism is to believe that it is not only possible for human beings of different faiths and race to live together in harmony, but that out of this diversity and sharing comes a special richness and vitality, and that this diversity is like the broad base to a pyramid, one of the best basic reasons for our faith in the enduring of our nation.

OUR NEW DEPARTMENT—
CHRISTIAN RELATIONS

by

Maurice Smith

A business man, sleepless, tossing in his Pull-
man berth, wonders if he has done everything pos-
sible to improve working conditions in his plant.
As a result, the Bristol Manufacturing Corpora
tion of Bristol, Rhode Island, inaugurates a truly
Christian experiment. Maurice C. Smith, Jr.,
president of the corporation, relates the fascinating
story of a new departure for a business concern.

"GOD IS OUR PARTNER" IS A REALITY IN THE BRISTOL MANUFAC-
turing Corporation.

Our plant recently created a new department—the Department
of Christian Relations. Its head and vice president of our company is Rev. Dale D. Dutton who resigned as Pastor of the Central
Baptist Church of Providence, R. I., to take the position.

This department will be devoted exclusively to the service of
God and to a policy of unselfishness. Our instructions to the Rev.
Dale D. Dutton are simply these, "Go about doing all the good
you can find to do in this world, and look to God for His leadership, not to the directors or officers of our company."

Three men are responsible for this venture: company treasurer
William H. Smith, who is my brother and who originally recommended the idea, Rev. Dale D. Dutton and myself.

First, some of the background. In 1931 a large plant in Bristol,

Rhode Island, closed, throwing many men and women out of work. I resigned my position with that company and attempted to organize a plant primarily to provide jobs for these unemployed men and women. The plan was unsuccessful. Disillusioned, I moved from Bristol determined to forget sentiment and make money. Soon I was doing just that in another business.

One Sunday I listened to a sermon that brought me up with a start. The minister (not Rev Dutton whom I did not meet until years later) seemed to look right into my eyes as he pointed out the responsibility and obligation that business men have toward workers and toward God.

"Any man who has the ability to organize and operate a business and thus provide employment must fulfill this obligation," the minister declared. "If such a man fails in this duty," he continued, "he will bump headlong into this scriptural passage: 'Inasmuch as ye have done it unto one of the least of these, my brethren, ye have done it unto *Me.*'"

I left the church that morning with my thoughts in a turmoil. There was no question about it. I had the ability to organize a plant and employ men. Was I failing in my obligations? Then I began to rationalize My present job was important. Times were bad. A new business involved too much risk. Soon I managed to explain away the whole sermon.

But the minister was not through with me. The following Sunday he again struck home with a devastating thrust. The subject of his talk was. "Emancipation from Fear." In a ringing voice he pronounced that man would never accomplish big objectives if he let fear dominate his thinking.

"But," he said, " a man who will take God as his partner will derive more help from this than from any earthly partnership. *One plus God is an army.*"

I sat rooted in my pew. God was never more real than at that moment. He was talking to me through this minister. He read the doubts in my mind. He was telling me to throw off my fears and strike out under His partnership. My obligations to Him and to my fellow men were outlined in terms that I could never explain away.

I returned to Bristol and organized a new plant with the help of the people of Bristol, many of whom became employees in this new enterprise. Progress was slow, competition keen, profits nonexistent for many years, but there was no question this time of quitting. My life's work was dedicated to helping the people of Bristol, 800 of whom are now employees in this plant.

My friendship with Rev. Dutton began in 1943. This friendship soon became rather turbulent because until recently we differed strenuously in many of our beliefs. Rev. Mr. Dutton is a dynamic man, a powerful Christian leader who has the ability to move people into action with his sermons. I felt that some of his ideas were wrong and selfishly wanted him to change over completely to my point of view.

God was never closer to me than during one period of coolness between Rev. Dutton and myself. I was very much worked up late one afternoon about something and decided to write him an overpoweringly critical letter.

I dictated the letter to my Ediphone. It was a bitter letter, and I left the cylinder for my stenographer to type the first thing in the morning.

When I arrived at my office the following morning, I discovered to my amazement that the cylinder was on the machine, the machine open for dictating and my stenographer and secretary were in my office.

"Mr. Smith," my secretary said, "the letter you dictated yesterday was only half recorded on the cylinder."

I was startled. How could this be? Yet it was true. Half of the letter was simply not recorded. "I will dictate the other half right away," I told her brusquely.

The phone rang. It was the Rev. Dutton!

"Maurice," he said, "I must see you today. We have important matters to discuss."

The Ediphone not recording might have been an accident. *But not this call at this particular moment!*

That night Mr. Dutton and I had a wonderful heart-warming discussion. We opened our hearts to each other, reconciled our differences and came to a great understanding. At the end we were on our knees before God thanking Him for preserving a wonderful friendship.

The idea for creating the Department of Christian Relations came from my brother. One night while tossing in a Pullman berth he reviewed the many steps our plant had taken to improve working and living conditions of employees and their families. In spite of all this, he could not help but feel that business as a whole was a selfish institution.

Would it be possible to create a department that would be entirely unselfish in character, a department dedicated to the service of others, not for the sale of more merchandise nor for publicity? He had in mind a department which would operate as did Jesus Christ nineteen hundred years ago when "He went about doing good."

Yes, there were departments for public relations, for human relations, for personnel relations. *Why not a department of Christian Relations under a man who was deeply spiritual and who had a passion for serving others?*

Upon his return to Bristol he discussed the matter with me, and while I liked the idea at once I felt that it called for much thought and prayer. For business it was a new idea. Would it be misunderstood? Would we receive criticism, possibly ridicule but, on the other hand, wouldn't the good resulting from it more than offset all the rest?

As soon as my brother finished outlining his idea I knew there was only one man for the job—Rev. Mr. Dutton. When he was offered the position he, too, recognized the challenge and the responsibility involved. The whole venture was so important to us all that it was several weeks before a final decision and agreement were reached.

Our first intention was to give absolutely no publicity to the department However, as soon as Mr. Dutton resigned his pastorate, the story broke and the resulting publicity was amazing. As we feared, many misunderstood our motives. We were congratulated on developing a smart publicity stunt and denounced as hypocrites in the same breath. Fortunately, many people believed in our sincerity and their letters have been heartwarming.

May I stress once more that this Department of Christian Relations was not intended to be publicized. It was not created to develop additional business. It was formed to further tolerance and unselfishness and to make Christ alive to men and women. Mr. Dutton is paid a salary, has an expense account and is supplied secretarial help. His department operates on a budget, sharing the successes and reverses of the company. If we find need for additional funds over and above his budget we feel that God will supply them by giving us these funds from outside sources.

Our plant has a Personnel Relations Department devoting its energies to the improvement of conditions and morale among employees. Mr. Dutton does not act as an industrial chaplain. Employees may come to him with their problems if they wish but they must take the initiative. His main job is outside our plant.

From the hundreds of letters which we have received it would appear that his course of action is fairly well charted. There have been some financial appeals, but for the most part there seems to be a yearning in the hearts of men and women for a deeper spiritual experience. As an official of a college put it, "We have lost our Christian idealism. Will you come and help us recover it?"

We are looking to God to develop our program because this happens to be one department of our company which is not humanly controlled. We hope that this idea of doing good will spread to other concerns and help business remove the stigma of selfishness.

RELIGION HELPS US COMBAT CRIME

by

Edward Thompson

*Lawbreakers can change into useful citizens.
Judge Edward Thompson, the youngest magistrate in New York City, dramatically illustrates
how the courts are helping offenders find a new
outlook on life.*

WHAT CAN BE DONE TODAY TO STOP THE INCREASE IN CRIME AND
lawlessness? The problem is so big and complex that there is no
one solution.

We in the courts are trying to do something about it—something in addition to adding more policemen to the force and convicting and sentencing more lawbreakers to institutions. Something much more difficult than all this!

We are trying to reach inside many offenders to help them find
a new self-respect and a new life as law-abiding citizens. To do
this we have to use weapons much more intangible than laws and
court orders. The needed inspiration and incentive to change
criminal ways won't necessarily come from man-made laws . . .

But from God!

Religion is the answer to reforming many habitual offenders.
The Church, as the oldest institution, *can* and *has* succeeded
where the courts have failed. Our new role is to see that the
Church has an opportunity to exert its healing influence on lawbreakers.

[246]

Take the case of Mary Smith. That isn't her real name, but her story is real and it happened very recently. She stood before me one day, her clothes wrinkled and dirty, a tired, sullen look in her eyes. The charge—disorderly conduct.

Glancing at her record my jaw dropped. It was fantastic. Mary Smith, fifty-four years old—with fifty-three previous convictions! The offenses, all minor, were generally the outcome of intoxication. She had served, among others, eight six-month sentences.

How could one human being so consistently degrade herself? Upon looking at her more closely, though, what I saw in her eyes was hopelessness, not an incurable vileness.

"Mary, what can I do for you?" I asked her kindly.

Something vague flickered in her eyes. "Judge, you can give me another chance."

Snickers drifted through the courtroom. Mary was well known as an oft-convicted offender. Her request seemed ironically funny.

"Mary," I continued, "tell me what is the difference between this occasion and all the others?"

"Judge, this time I'm in love."

Outright laughter greeted this surprising statement. The idea of tawdry, unkempt Mary in love seemed ludicrous at that moment. I felt sorry for her, but the situation was not without humor.

"Who is the lucky man?" I asked gently.

"Mr. Otto Schmidt," she said after some hesitation.

More smirks from the now interested court. For the first time, however, there was a new spirit in Mary's eyes as she flashed a defiant glance about her. The mention of this man's name roused her from her apathy.

I frowned over my court with rising resentment. Mary might be a hopeless offender, but she was a human being with feelings, and I did not intend to let any atmosphere of levity trample her spirit.

"Mary, is Mr. Schmidt in the court?" I asked.

In reply a tall, elderly man arose and moved forward, causing a new buzz of comment. Mr. Schmidt, a gentleman in his seventies, was well dressed with a poised, distinguished appearance.

The case was becoming more interesting by the minute.

As Mary saw Mr. Schmidt coming forward she began to smooth down her untidy hair in some agitation. Something in his eyes suddenly seemed to reassure her, however, and her shoulders straightened.

"Mr. Schmidt," I began, "Mary has stated that she is in love with you, that because of this love she would like another opportunity to prove she can become a good citizen. How do you feel about this?"

"I have loved Mary for three years now. She is no criminal," he said simply.

"Then why did you let her commit this offense?"

"I was away on a business trip. Judge, if you will check the records, you will notice that this is her first arrest during the past three years."

I looked over Mary's record again. It was astoundingly true! Then I noticed a real look of hope on Mary's face—and something else in her eyes as she gazed fondly at the dignified man beside her.

"Judge," Mary interrupted suddenly, "there is another reason why I want another chance. My boy is due back from the Pacific next week. I want to be free to welcome him home."

Here was another consideration. Could it be a play for my sympathy? I conferred with the probation officer, a court veteran, well familiar with Mary's past performances. He was unmoved. To him Mary was a menace to society, an incurable alcoholic. His recommendation—the same as before, a prison sentence. Based on the law and her record, he was indubitably correct.

A woman with fifty-three previous convictions certainly didn't seem like a fit subject for probation. Frankly, I was reluctant to go out on a limb for Mary, yet what possible good would another prison sentence do? I felt that any person who had the capacity for love could not be incorrigibly bad. Suddenly I knew that the only possible way of salvaging Mary was to give her a chance to do it herself.

"Mary," I said, "your boy made a great sacrifice for you and for all of us by serving overseas. Don't you think he has repaid you for the sacrifices you made for him? Don't you think it would make him very unhappy if he could see you now?"

"Oh, yes, Judge."

"Mary, I'm going to put you on indefinite probation because I believe you can and will become a good citizen. But there are several things I want you to do. First, you must give up drinking. Give it up completely. This sacrifice is certainly small in comparison to that of your son's."

She nodded vigorously.

"The other thing I want you to do," I continued, "is to go to church regularly and give God a chance to help you overcome your desire for alcohol. You may not realize it, but loving Mr. Schmidt and your son has brought you very close to God. Now try going to church—loving God—and see if it doesn't help you find a new self-respect and happiness."

Tears spilled over Mary's shabby clothes as she thanked me. Then she clasped her hands together—and I saw her lips move in a quiet prayer.

During the weeks that followed I was able to get regular and accurate reports on Mary through our efficient probation system. Each one filled me with increased hope and confidence in the wisdom of my decision. Mary was not only going to church regularly, but she was participating in other church activities. Skeptical court officials, however, were unimpressed and figured it was only a matter of time. I kept my fingers crossed because her complete reform meant more to me than I cared to admit.

I had pinned my hopes on a powerful ally in religion, though. I was sure that if Mary took an active part in church life, as the reports stated she was doing, she would feel the effects in her own life. For living close to God inevitably brings on cleanliness, both of body and mind, in addition to self-respect.

Several months later I returned from another assignment. The court attendant greeted me in my office. "Mary was back," he deadpanned.

Something seemed to sag inside me, then came a sharp sense of futility. "I guess I should have known better than to let her off," I said unhappily.

"Oh, she wasn't locked up. She came just to see you."

"To see me!"

"That's right. We didn't recognize her at first. Mary had on new clothes and looked like a million. She had the Probation Department's okey to go out West with her new husband—that Mr. Schmidt—but she wanted to thank you again before leaving."

"And Judge," said the attendant with a knowing wink, "she said she wanted to kiss you good-bye!"

I laughed happily. The feeling of futility was gone.

All such cases naturally do not have happy ending, but more and more do each day. Most of the offenders are bewildered, unsettled people who need only a start in the right direction to overcome their criminal tendencies. Here is where religion can be of tremendous help. Some cases we assign directly to a clergyman. Others like Mary need only to be headed back to the church. Then, of course, some need considerable psychiatric treatment.

But the great dynamic cure comes from God.

HOW CHRISTIANITY
CAN WORK IN
YOUR COMMUNITY

by

George Stoll

Congregations should certainly do more than congregate! So thought George Stoll one Sunday morning while coming out of church. Roused into action, Mr. Stoll, president of the Stoll Oil Refining Company, gathered together a group of Louisville churchmen and fired them with his enthusiasm. The work of the resulting Committee on Institutions of the Louisville Council of Churches has produced a new youth center, improved jail conditions and bettered local government.

JIMMY DOREMI WAS FLIRTING WITH TROUBLE AGAIN.

Jimmy, age thirteen, listened with glistening eyes to two older boys—much older boys—of fifteen. They were planning to steal a car. Jimmy trembled with excitement.

A policeman strolled down the street and eyed the three boys as they slouched against the dirty windows of the pool hall. Troublemakers. He could tell by their furtive expressions.

Jimmy's excitement cooled at the sight of the policeman. Suddenly stealing a car didn't seem so smart after all. He remembered too well his last bitter experience with the law. Dared to swipe a tire from O'Toole's garage, he had been caught and brought before the Judge. The Judge had lectured him sternly, then warned that the next offense would be dealt with severely. Jimmy winced as he remembered the beating his father had given him.

There is no real Jimmy Doremi, but police records show that there were many idle and confused boys like Jimmy. Not really bad boys. Just kids who had a lot of steam to let off and no place to do it. There was a lot of this in one Louisville district. It wasn't a bad district. But ninety-two arrests of juveniles had occurred in a radius of six blocks in six months!

While the restless Jimmies of this area were plotting their adventure, another group was doing some plotting. This group was plotting to develop better conditions. A group of Louisville churchmen—a lawyer and four businessmen—met with the officers of the Salvation Army. They were concerned about a community center that had been closed. The property belonged to the First Christian Church. They came out of this meeting with four objectives:

1. To get permission of the First Christian Church to use the property as a Boys' Club.
2. To get a qualified person who would give the Club full time to direct its activities.
3. To go with the Salvation Army before the Community Chest to secure sufficient funds to operate.
4. To outline a program that would be effective on boys from the age of seven to seventeen, that would build character, teach fair play and obedience to the law.

All the objectives were reached within a reasonable time and within a short period the Club was in operation. In the first year nearly 300 members came in. It has grown steadily each year since that time.

This had taken time and plenty of hard work, but a flourishing Boys' Club complete with playroom, billiard table, ping pong table, a wood-working shop and a library, was operating. Kids like Jimmy Doremi no longer had to roam the streets to let off steam.

In the last six months there has not been a single juvenile arrest in that area. The Crime Prevention Bureau gives the Boys' Club full credit for this splendid record.

The small group, headed by Fred Vawter, a lawyer, which quietly worked out this program is a division of the Committee on Institutions of the Louisville Council of Churches. The Committee comprises two hundred Louisville churchmen who have found a way to translate practical Christianity into practical government.

Our organization has sub-committees which study jails, courts, hospitals, public homes and child-caring institutions After observing conditions and comparing practices with those in other states, we launch projects to help management improve conditions.

I have always felt that congregations should do more than congregate. Back in 1940, when the Committee was first appointed, I discovered there were others who felt the same way. Too many people were coming out of church with the remark: "I've heard many splendid sermons just like that one They inspire you to do something for your fellow man, but somebody should tell us what to do and how to do it."

This set me to thinking.

During the next weeks I made the rounds of other churches, talked with ministers and from them got the names of those who might be interested in committee work to help improve conditions in our community. The response was encouraging. We formed one committee, then another

From the first we realized that we had to plan and organize very carefully or suffer the fate of other similar drives which start with enthusiasm and fall apart from sheer inefficiency and incoherence. Above all, study was necessary before any action could be taken. The emphasis is on co-operation rather than criticism.

Our work is completely divorced from politics. We do point out a bad system or public apathy, however, if that is where the fault lies.

We begin with the assumption that every office-holder would rather do a good job than a poor one. Rather than rebuke, we start by finding something to commend The handicaps that public officials work under are well-known: lack of funds, poor equipment and lack of trained personnel.

Our Bible keynote is taken from the twenty-fifth chapter of Matthew, verses 31-46: "I was a stranger, and ye took me in: Naked and ye clothed me. I was sick, and ye visited me: I was in prison, and ye came unto me."

Our county jail was long a decrepit lock-up. It was frequently criticized in the local press. We invited the jailer to come to our Jail Committee meeting He came. In fact he joined the Committee and was a regular and faithful attendant. He was not happy over jail conditions He was delighted to find a group that would see problems eye to eye with him. He stated frankly that after a stay in jail, except for drunks sent in to sober up, a man left the jail worse than when he came in. But what could the jailer do?

One week-end the Committee members set up a constant two-man vigil at the jail. Working in six-hour shifts from Saturday midnight until the next Monday morning, the two-man teams observed the complete jail routine. We also stationed members at the hold-over, where arrests are slated, as well as at the hospital where accident cases were brought.

By the time we had completed a full study of conditions, a political change had brought in a new jailer. We began to work with him He cleaned up the jail. He not only cleaned up the physical jail, he took interest in the prisoners. Books, magazines were sent in, pastors were encouraged to visit prisoners, and entertainment was scheduled

Who received the credit? The jailer, of course. He deserved it. As far as we were concerned the improvements were there. That's all that matters.

Mere improvements were not quite enough. A long range program was planned to get rid of the jail and workhouse, replacing them with a prison farm There food and surroundings would be better, prisoners would have work and costs would be cut.

One of the most significant accomplishments of our work has been the development of lay leaders. Psychiatrists, public officials, wardens, insurance men and business men as well as ministers have rolled up their sleeves and pitched into this "Christianity of Doing" with real enthusiasm. Tapping these professional men for our projects in practical Christian citizenship is the source of our strength.

Ours is a project in Kingdom promotion. It starts with the idea that the church is important, but that congregations should do more than congregate! Rather, "Every member a minister, and the clergyman a coach." And always the question: "What would Christ have done in this situation?"

Remember—those divided in creeds can be united in deeds.

CPSIA information can be obtained
at www.ICGtesting.com
Printed in the USA
LVOW13s0726240518
578348LV00013B/449/P